Advance Praise

"Dr. Catherine Xiang's book is a must-read for a [...] *China. In a* 蜻蜓点水 *world that basks in the supe* [...] *touches the water surface), this book dives deep w.* [...] *of detail and soars high with overarching explanations of the causes of things. In a world where most books are dragonflies, this book is a dragon!"*
George Iliev, MBA (伊乔),
China Director, Association of MBAs (AMBA)

"Forget fumbling in the fog of cultural confusion and dry business guild! Bridging the Gap hands you the key to mastering intercultural communication and helps you navigate the wild world of doing business in China. Say hello to smooth cross-cultural convos in the business world!"
Arnold Ma
CEO, Qumin and Dao Insights

"Catherine Xiang proves once again her unparalleled expertise in inter-cultural communication between East and West. This book helps business leaders, executives and other key stakeholders better understand the complexities of the Chinese culture and navigate the philosophical and cultural underpinnings. It is an essential guide to succeed in the Chinese market and make a long-lasting, positive and sustainable impact for the generations to come."
Martina Fuchs
Business Journalist, China & Middle East Expert,
Board Member, Montreux Jazz Festival China

"I thoroughly recommend Bridging the Gap. As a social anthropology graduate, I am impressed with the quality of Catherine's insights into the depth of Chinese culture, and the complexities and challenges of inter-cultural communication. This is an enjoyable read, and Catherine helps the reader gain a much better understanding of Chinese culture."
Sarah Chidgey
Head of International Education,
Department for Business and Trade (DBT)

"This book takes as its central theme the close interconnections between language, culture and communication. This is a vitally important perspective for all intercultural interaction, and especially so for China, where the language and its foundations are so different from European languages. Those doing business with China will find within the book a wealth of source ideas for reflection and application, including very helpful background information on the Chinese language, Chinese cultural key words, Chinese philosophical traditions and values, and key features of Chinese communication patterns."

Professor Helen Spencer-Oatey
Emeritus Professor, University of Warwick

"Intercultural communication is critically important to understand how we relate to each other in an increasingly complex geopolitical landscape. Catherine Hua Xiang provides us with the tools and the strategies for a more nuanced cross-cultural interaction with China. Bridging the gap between theory and practice, the book will be extremely useful for students, scholars and businesspeople alike, leading them with clear, connected and comfortable steps into a tango of language, culture and successful interaction with the Chinese universe."

Professor Maurizio Marinelli
Professor of China and Global Prosperity,
University College London

"Depending upon where you are born in the world, you will have a unique idea about right and wrong. The truth in a globalized world is, however, that you form your opinion through 'coloured glass' that determines your actions and form of execution, which most likely will lead to a non-desired result. To succeed in China, it's crucial to understand who you are addressing and thus through which 'coloured glass' they form their opinions and approaches. Bridging the Gap, by helping you understand the 'what,' 'why' and 'how,' is essential reading for achieving fruitful outcomes and effective communication with China."

Hans Henrik Pontoppidan
Secretary General of Danish-Chinese Business Forum

"In Bridging the Gap, *Catherine Hua Xiang opens a window into the language of a country whose culture and history are second to none. Using an engaging style that combines the key theoretical concepts with extremely practical everyday examples, Catherine Hua Xiang brilliantly illustrates how mastering cultural context is essential in order to avoid getting literally lost in translation. Understanding the concept of face, differences in Chinese vs. Western values systems (collective vs. individual, short- vs. long-term orientation, direct vs. indirect approaches), as well as the etiquette (hierarchy and protocol, the importance of relationship building) can be the difference between success and failure in communicating with Chinese counterparts. If you have to choose one book to help you master the foundations of successful intercultural communication in Chinese – this is the one."*
Matei Negrescu
Vice President, Renewables Strategy at Equinor

"Language is more than just words; talking is more than just speaking. When trying to communicate in a different environment, understanding even the basic foundations of the culture can make the difference in successful intercultural relations. Catherine Hua Xiang deftly builds bridges between Chinese and Western culture effectively in this book series by introducing the reader to the differences in philosophy and approach to language in China, and explains the whys and hows of better communication practice. An enlightening read that makes what can seem inexplicable at times so much clearer."
Professor Ian Baxter
Professor of Historic Environment Management,
Heriot-Watt University

"This valuable book provides many fascinating insights to navigate the highly nuanced communication dynamics within Chinese culture. With its blend of wisdom and practical advice, readers will enhance their cultural fluency and agility, fostering stronger relationships essential for successful business ventures bridging the West and China."
Professor Keith Jackson
Export Champion

Published by
LID Publishing
An imprint of LID Business Media Ltd.
LABS House, 15–19 Bloomsbury Way,
London, WC1A 2TH, UK

info@lidpublishing.com
www.lidpublishing.com

A member of:

businesspublishersroundtable.com

© Dr Catherine Hua Xiang, 2024
© LID Business Media Limited, 2024
Reprinted in 2024

Printed and bound in Great Britain by Halstan Ltd
ISBN: 978-1-915951-04-5
ISBN: 978-1-915951-05-2 (ebook)

Cover and page design: Caroline Li

Bridging the Gap

AN INTRODUCTION TO INTERCULTURAL COMMUNICATION WITH CHINA

Dr Catherine Hua Xiang

MADRID | MEXICO CITY | LONDON
BUENOS AIRES | BOGOTA | SHANGHAI

Contents

Preface

For two decades, my career has been deeply entrenched in the nuances of intercultural communication between China and the West. Every facet of my life revolves around this unique dance of cultures. As a native of Shanghai, my daily life in the UK is filled with interactions with 'foreigners', both professionally and personally.

In 2011, I became a part of the esteemed London School of Economics and Political Science (LSE). LSE, often dubbed the 'little UN', is renowned for the diverse linguistic and cultural backgrounds of its students. This claim isn't mere hyperbole – as the programme director of BSc International Relations and Chinese, I vividly recall stepping into a class-room where each of the 12 students hailed from a distinct nation. Truly captivating!

The LSE Language Centre, where I serve, is perhaps the most multilingual and multicultural hub at LSE. We offer instruction in nine languages, with my remit covering East Asian languages, encompassing Mandarin, Japanese and Korean. I also engage in collaborative projects with colleagues who teach other languages. To me, engaging with those from different backgrounds is an endless source of learning and skill refinement. Successful cross-cultural communication often requires deep, real-life experiences to grasp the subtleties.

I am also the UK Director of the Confucius Institute for Business London (CIBL), a collaborative endeavour between LSE and Tsinghua University, China. At CIBL, our emphasis lies in teaching professionals the intricacies of business-focused Chinese education and intercultural communication between China and the UK. Whether it's discussing matters with the vice president of Tsinghua University or liaising with a significant corporate client in London, my role demands an agile cultural switch. This continual adaptation and the need for deep cultural insight isn't without its challenges, even for a veteran like me.

My lessons in intercultural communication aren't confined to the office. At home, I share my life with an Italian, who, in jest, I say behaves more like a German. No slight intended bias toward Germans, and I recognize the pitfalls of such generalizations. But such intercultural interactions, even miscommunications, often lend a humorous touch. Our occasional disagreements provide a mirror to reflect on the broader subject of intercultural communication and my cultural identity. Much to his chagrin, I often correlate our discussions with established theories in intercultural communication. In lighter moments, he quips about my supposed 'expertise.'

There is a gap in Western understanding of Chinese communication nuances. The global dialogue around China often zeroes in on economy and politics, side-lining the richness of its language and societal dynamics. This oversight is unfortunate; communication underpins everything we do. To foster meaningful exchanges and thriving relationships, understanding language and its cultural backdrop is paramount. This is the essence of this book, which delves into the heart of understanding Chinese communication norms.

As the inaugural book in a series centred on effective communication and fostering relationships through linguistic and cultural sensitivity, it seeks to offer a holistic overview of the 'what,' 'why' and 'how.' By its conclusion, I aim for you to:

- Grasp the distinct traits of Chinese communication
- Comprehend why the Chinese communicate as they do
- Learn effective strategies for business communication with the Chinese

We commence with the observable – the 'what.' In Part One, I shed light on the common hurdles in intercultural communication with China and underscore salient differences in communication styles. As we delve deeper, I urge you to juxtapose my insights with your experiences. Our exploration will then pivot to the 'why,' unveiling the cultural bedrock of Chinese communication. And to round off, we'll delve into the 'how,' offering tools and strategies for successful cross-cultural interactions.

Both my professional and personal worlds consistently challenge, invigorate and refine my understanding of intercultural communication – a vibrant dance of language, culture and interaction. This interplay motivated me to pen this book. The art of communication, and the underlying cultural factors, is both intriguing and vital to master. It offers us a chance to broaden our horizons and cultivate a more open-minded worldview.

Are you prepared for this enlightening journey? Let's go.

Introduction

The stars of the new global economic order were barely glinting as the dawn of the 21st century spread around the world. But even then, one star was already on its course to outshine them all – China.

It is a story of unparalleled growth and influence. It is a story of a nation that, in just a few decades, lifted hundreds of millions of people from poverty and positioned itself as the world's second-largest economy. It is a story of relentless determination, profound adaptability and sheer economic force.

And it is a story that is intimately entwined with our own.

Imagine standing on the edge of a cliff, looking out onto a sprawling landscape of vast potential. You are aware of the priceless treasures that lie on the other side, but between you and the treasures is a deep, wide, often turbulent sea. You must traverse this sea to reach the wealth waiting on the other side.

In the landscape of global economics, China is that land of abundant treasure. The sea that separates us, that is the barrier to this treasure, is the challenge of communication. The language, the culture, the deeply ingrained philosophies of the East, all form part of this complex matrix.

China's economy is not just any treasure island; it is a vast continent of opportunity. With a GDP standing at more than $14 trillion, China's economic power is second only to the United States. It is the world's largest exporter, the second-largest importer, and home to some of the biggest multinational corporations. These are not just dry statistics; they are an open invitation to engage, collaborate and thrive.

During an interview with CGTN anchor Guan Xin in early 2023, McKinsey China Chairman Joe Ngai's remarked "The next China is China" and it went viral. He highlighted the resilience of China's economy which, despite global challenges, is expected to contribute a significant chunk to global growth. While developed markets are showing a GDP growth of around 1.5–2.5% and emerging markets around 3.5–4.5%, China's projected 5% GDP growth stands out, underscoring its vital role in the global economy. Six months later, in November 2023, Ngai reaffirmed his views, stating that he is even more convinced by his initial observations.

OK, hold on a second. Please don't get confused. This book is not about statistics, charts and economic theories. It's about understanding, bridging gaps and forging connections. It's about the importance of effectively communicating with China and why doing so is crucial in the landscape of today's interconnected world.

Failing to communicate effectively is costly. The cost implications of intercultural miscommunication are often overlooked, yet research indicates that cultural differences lead to communication breakdowns in international trade, particularly with China's trade relations. A 2020 study examined how ICT development and intercultural miscommunication interact, and their combined impact on international trade. Having analysed 10 years of bilateral trade data between China and 29 of its major trading partners, the study found that intercultural miscommunication negatively affected trade, diminishing the positive impact of ICT development. Regression analysis revealed that a 1% increase in intercultural miscommunication could lead to a 0.77% decrease in trade volume. This is a price you wouldn't want to pay!

As the ancient Chinese proverb goes, "If you want to be rich, you must first build roads." Today, those roads are made not just of concrete and steel but also of words and understanding. So, let's build those roads together, by exploring the potential, understanding the challenges and creating pathways to effective communication with China.

ACKNOWLEDGING THE GAP IN OUR LINGUISTIC AND CULTURAL UNDERSTANDING

If the economic argument is not enough to convince you, let's address the importance of understanding effective communication with China from a different perspective. We live in a diverse world with hundreds of languages spoken around the globe. However, not all languages share the same number of users and impact. English is the most spoken language around the world but as a first language, Chinese takes the lead. The Chinese language is spoken by nearly 1.2 billion people as their native language, followed by 399 million Spanish native speakers. English only comes third and there are about 335 million native English speakers. With almost a fifth of the world's population speaking Chinese, without knowing this language and culture, you are missing much understanding and therefore many opportunities.

However, English continues to be the most studied language in the world. According to the *South China Morning Post* in 2015, approximately 1,500 million people worldwide are learning English. French remains a popular language and Chinese is catching up, with around 30 million people learning the language, overtaking traditional European languages such as Spanish and German. In China, the number of learners of English continues to grow. In 2018, it was more than 400 million – more than the population of the United States.

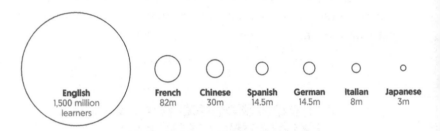

English
1,500 million
learners

French
82m

Chinese
30m

Spanish
14.5m

German
14.5m

Italian
8m

Japanese
3m

MOST POPULAR LANGUAGE BEING
LEARNED AROUND THE WORLD

Let's put the above numbers into some perspective. To simplify the maths, we take 400 million Chinese leaners of English from the 1,500 million total learners in total, meaning 30% of the world's English learners are Chinese. The ratio between Chinese learners of English versus native English speaker is 1.26, whereas the ratio between Mandarin learners in the entire world and native Chinese speakers is 0.025. This is a huge gap.

It's not solely about the total number of learners but also about their profiles. In China, the age of English learners is steadily decreasing. English is compulsory in primary schools, and many children begin learning English as early as nursery. Chinese parents invest significantly in their children's English abilities and experiences of studying abroad. They believe that being bilingual confers a unique advantage. This learner profile signals the future of China and its populace – bilingual and, arguably, as a result, with a sound understanding of Western culture and society.

If the Chinese are dedicating time and effort to learn about English and the West, how does the West reciprocate? We don't seem to exhibit the same degree of eagerness and interest. According to *The Times*, there's a shortage of Mandarin speakers in the UK, causing concern for future diplomacy: "Only 14 Foreign Office officials are being trained to speak fluent Mandarin each year on average, a transparency request reveals, raising concerns for future diplomacy. (20 Aug 2022)." I'm sure you'd agree that this number isn't impressive in the slightest. Language is one aspect; the other is cultural knowledge. Let's examine the two images below.

MONA LISA BY LEONARDO DA VINCI

THE RIVERSIDE SCENE AT QINGMING FESTIVAL, 清明上河图,
BY ZHANG ZEDUAN

I'm sure you can identify the name and artist of the first painting. If you were to ask a Chinese university student, I'm confident they could do the same and even explain the significance of the artwork. Some may have even seen it in person at the Louvre. But how many of you can identify the second painting? If you can't, don't be disheartened. Many of my highly educated students, undertaking a joint degree with Chinese at the London School of Economics and Political Science, were also unaware. Ironically, the second painting is one of the most renowned paintings in China, often referred to as "China's Mona Lisa." This painting is titled "清明上河图," translated as "The Riverside Scene at Qingming Festival," from the Song Dynasty. It depicts the daily life of people and the landscape of the capital, Bianjing (modern-day Kaifeng), during the Northern Song period. This handscroll painting was created by Zhang Zeduan. Its archaeological significance is unique; as one unrolls it from left to right, successive scenes reveal the lifestyles across societal strata, from the affluent to the underprivileged. It also provides insights into economic activities in both rural and urban settings, showcasing period clothing and architecture.

While we shouldn't expect everyone to become experts in Chinese history and art, having a basic understanding is a gesture of respect toward your Chinese colleagues. The Chinese are always appreciative, even if you offer a simple greeting like "你好" (Nǐ hǎo, hello). As Nelson Mandela once famously said, "If you talk to a man in a language he understands, that goes to his head. If you talk to him in his language, that goes to his heart."

Becoming acquainted with China enables you to establish rapport and possess the necessary understanding to engage or compete effectively. Based on data and my personal observations, I perceive a disparity between how the Chinese learn about the West and the Western approach to understanding China. This gap needs to be closed.

CHINESE COMMUNICATION IS DIFFERENT FROM WESTERN COUNTRIES

If we all thought and communicated in the same manner, one might think the world would be a harmonious place. In reality, it would just be rather monotonous. Linguistic and cultural diversity provides us with opportunities to learn, to appreciate varied perspectives and to cultivate wisdom. China stands apart. Its language, patterns of thought and philosophical foundations have evolved differently from those of the West. Consequently, it's only natural that its modes of communication will also differ. But to what extent? And what are the reasons behind these differences?

Let's start with some stories based on real events.

There is No Rush

Beijing, in all its vibrant bustle, posed a formidable challenge to Miss Jiang, an American-born Chinese architect, as she found herself lost in the labyrinthine business culture of China. She hoped to showcase her design for a house for older people, but the task seemed steeped in mystery, wrapped in a complex tapestry of Chinese social etiquette and local customs.

In a high-stakes meeting with two powerhouses, Manager Luo and Director Ma, she found herself caught in a whirlwind of rapid Mandarin, laced with nuances that escaped her grasp. Manager Luo is a significant figure in Beijing's business milieu and the developer for her project, and Director Ma is the director of the local planning office. To her surprise and annoyance, the conversation was more a lyrical dance of compliments and less a discussion about her architectural vision.

The exchange seemed to continue forever. Each compliment, each reference to Chinese history and literature, felt like a further divergence from the reason she was there. Yet, Miss Jiang felt compelled to listen, to try to understand the rhythm of this unfamiliar dance. She couldn't understand why they kept calling each other brothers. The staff even compared Director Ma to the "buffet in the government."

Manager Luo turned to Director Ma and said, "Brother, if one day you wish to start your own business, our company would be honoured to support you. I would happily step down to assist you."

Liang's patience was wearing thin. The meeting deviated further and further from her plans. Subtly, she interjected, "Mr. Luo, may we discuss my proposal?" However, Luo redirected the conversation to Director Ma, seeking his opinion on her project. Ma's didn't say "yes" or "'no." Instead, all he said was that providing housing to elderly was the type of venture that the government would look to support.

Manager Luo was all smiles. The seemingly positive response was a balm to Liang's rising frustration, but why couldn't he just give a straight answer? However, the cultural ritual was far from over. Manager Luo suggested she make a toast to Director Ma. Never a drinker, she hesitated before saying, "Sorry, I don't drink." Luo, insistent, prompted her to go ahead.

The clinking of glasses and the sound of laughter filled the room as Director Ma filled Liang's glass. She raised her glass with a mixture of hope and frustration. The cultural exchange, the compliment-laden conversations, were far from her comfort zone. But she understood that this was just the beginning of her journey into the fascinating world of Chinese business culture, a journey she was determined to navigate successfully.

Two meetings, two results

Stepping into the operations director role at a British firm, James felt as though he was navigating a ship through rough waters on a starless night. His unease stemmed from two business meetings with Chinese delegations that did not go as he had foreseen.

The first meeting hosted a group of six Chinese engineers. As he walked into the conference room, James's tie felt tight, mirroring the tension in his stomach. The chairman, the sales and marketing manager for China, was absent, leading to an awkward silence. Trying to alleviate the discomfort, James remarked, "Beautiful weather we're having. Certainly more pleasant than our usual British drizzle." The engineers nodded politely, and a light chuckle momentarily eased the atmosphere.

Hoping to further the dialogue, James inquired about their flight. One engineer praised the direct routes, and another shared a comical tale about in-flight meals, eliciting laughter from the group. As time ticked by, conversations shifted to the city's architecture and food. While James felt the minutes wasting away, the engineers, in contrast, seemed comfortable, adapting seamlessly to the delay. He was unaware then that these casual chats held deeper cultural implications.

In contrast, the second meeting, supervised by another operations director unfamiliar with China, seemed to be more efficient. The Chinese attendees, engineers with sales roles, had recently secured a significant deal for the firm. James expected a relaxed, grateful atmosphere.

However, the meeting morphed into a maze of cultural missteps. The Chinese delegates seemed to seek an equal status. Minor aspects, like seating or the meeting's flow, perturbed them. One even commented on the English attendees as being "commanding, contemptuous." James was taken aback. Wasn't this standard business practice?

The tipping point came when the interpreter halted the Chinese delegates from giving a counter-speech. Their evident disappointment left James disoriented. Why was this speech so pivotal?

Despite its initial awkwardness, the first meeting seemed to resonate more with the Chinese. The second, though streamlined, led to unexpected friction. James felt out of depth, like he was deciphering an unfamiliar script. The emphasis on 'equal status' and surprising focus on protocol left him puzzled and frustrated.

The Magical Sesame Biscuits

The business meeting John had just attended was unlike any he'd experienced. Accustomed to the conventional protocols of business interactions, he'd found this encounter bewilderingly tangential, yet oddly intimate. The conversation continued to replay in his mind.

"Mr. Zeng, should we schedule another meeting for further discussions?" he initiated, trying to establish some direction.

"That sounds good and beneficial," Mr. Zeng, the senior Chinese manager, replied. From there, the conversation strayed from the business-oriented discussions John was familiar with.

Suddenly, they were discussing supermarkets in Kent and the unique texture of sesame biscuits. Between the snippets of personal experiences and persistent recommendations to try these exceptionally crunchy biscuits, John found himself increasingly engrossed in these seemingly random tales.

The conversation leaped from a trip they took to his country in the early '90s to an in-depth dive into the health benefits of sesame seeds. He tried to redirect the conversation back to the primary agenda a few times, only to be gently sidetracked by another story.

"So, we're reconvening tomorrow?" he sought clarification.

"We have dinner planned for tonight at six-thirty. We'll meet at the hotel tomorrow," Mr. Zeng informed him. As the dialogue progressed, he grew acutely aware of being outside his usual business milieu.

The conversation wrapped up with chuckles. Even though the meeting's course had left him befuddled, John felt reassured that the business deal was sealed in this unorthodox manner. Somehow, it had worked. There was a certain charm embedded in the 'sesame biscuits' conversation, a reflection of the intricate ballet of cultural interactions, personal anecdotes and shared amusement.

These anecdotes illuminate some of the perplexities and frustrations that arise when interacting with Chinese counterparts in business settings. You might find these scenarios baffling, or perhaps they resonate with your own experiences – we often judge what deviates from our norms and values without truly grasping the nuances of the other culture. A mutual curiosity exists among all parties. The challenge arises from a gap in understanding, a gap that causes cultural missteps in communication. This book aims to bridge that gap. It furnishes you with a roadmap, aiding you in navigation and highlighting areas ripe for exploration. Furthermore, it points out the pitfalls, encouraging mindfulness on your journey. The cornerstone of this book is to foster intercultural awareness. By its conclusion, you will not only possess a deeper knowledge of China but, crucially, a clearer understanding of your own cultural identity. The most effective way to discern similarities or differences is by comparing them with something intimately familiar – namely, your own language, culture, and your ingrained ways of thinking and acting.

HOW TO USE THIS BOOK

This book unfolds over three distinct sections.

PART ONE: THE 'WHAT'

We begin with an in-depth exploration of the intricate relationships among language, culture and communication. This is followed by an introduction of the Chinese language. We then delve into the Chinese thought patterns, examine Chinese communication styles and investigate digital communication practices in China. This section takes you on a journey of discovery, encouraging you to engage with, and reflect upon, the diverse ways in which we think and communicate across cultures.

PART TWO: THE 'WHY'

The 'why' addresses the foundational reasons behind the phenomena observed in Part One. In this segment, you will explore the beliefs that underpin Chinese communication, the core values of Chinese culture and the impact of key cultural words in China. This essential background will offer you a deeper understanding of the cultural nuances that shape communication.

PART THREE: THE 'HOW'

In the final section, we turn to practical applications. Here, you are equipped with linguistic strategies and practical tools to apply your newfound knowledge in your professional and business interactions. We discuss navigating common challenges in intercultural communication, mastering intercultural communicative competence, adapting your communication style and engaging effectively with Chinese counterparts. Furthermore, we explore the building of successful international relations and rapport with the Chinese, and conclude with a chapter that contextualizes cultural complexity, helping you avoid oversimplification and stereotypes.

OK. It's time to dive in.

PART ONE

The 'What'

CHAPTER 1

Foundations Unveiled: Grasping the Basics

Before diving into the world of Chinese language and cultural complexities, it's pivotal to establish a solid foundational understanding of how language, culture and communication works. Just as an architect requires a firm grasp of the basic principles before designing a magnificent structure, our exploration of Chinese cultural dynamics demands a clear comprehension of certain elementary concepts. This chapter will unfold three fundamental pillars that are paramount to understanding global cultural interactions: cultural models, the role of language in shaping thought, and the diverse tapestry of communication styles around the globe. With a solid understanding of these basics, we'll be well-equipped to travel further into the intriguing maze of Chinese communication.

VOYAGES THROUGH CULTURAL LANDSCAPES: DECIPHERING COMMON MODELS

Culture has always been a complex tapestry woven from countless threads – beliefs, customs, values, behaviours and symbols. Through the ages, scholars have attempted to unravel this fascinating design to understand societies and the people who inhabit them. To simplify and visualize the dense intricacy of culture, several models have been proposed. Like maps guiding travellers through foreign terrains, these models help us navigate the rich landscapes of cultural contexts. Three such models – The Iceberg Model by Hall (1976), The Onion Model by Hofstede (2005), and the Cultural Glasses Model by Boas (1887) – provide foundational understandings of culture's depths, layers and perceptions. Let's look at each of them in turn.

1. The Iceberg Model: Beneath the Surface of Visibility

In 1976, the visionary anthropologist Edward T. Hall introduced the world to a profound analogy about the essence of culture. He depicted the complex and multifaceted culture of a society as an iceberg, a massive body with a deceptive nature. The visible part of the iceberg, looming above the water's surface, represented certain aspects of culture, those that are readily observable. However, the larger, hidden expanse submerged beneath the water signified the more profound and complex aspects of culture, often concealed from the initial observer's eye.

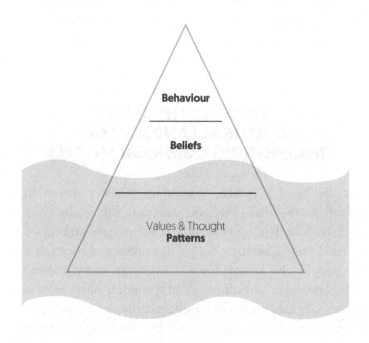

ICEBERG MODEL

According to Hall, only 10% of our culture is observable, such as what we wear, the food we eat and the language we speak. In other words, these are the 'what' part of the culture.

And the other 90% of our culture is not observable, such as our beliefs, core values, tradition and philosophy. Yet these aspects are largely influenced by history, geography and economy, as well as religion. They are the 'why' part of the culture and help explain why we wear the clothes we wear, eat the food we eat and speak the language we speak. No wonder understanding culture is hard; success depends on understanding the unseen.

The behaviour of different cultures may appear less foreign and threatening with an understanding of their worldviews, motivations, religious beliefs, attitudes to rules and other cultural orientations. To help you understand Chinese culture, this book will follow a similar logic, starting with the more visible aspects before moving toward the less visible.

2. The Onion Model: Peeling Back the Layers

Culture is one of those words that carries several meanings. Dutch social psychologist Professor Greet Hofstede defined it as: *The programming of the human mind by which one group of people distinguishes itself from another group.* Culture is learned from your environment and is always a shared, collective phenomenon.

According to Hofstede, the diverse facets of culture are likened to an onion: detailed and layered, with each tier revealing more about its inherent nature.

The outermost layers of this cultural onion are made up of tangible elements – artefacts, products and noticeable behaviour patterns. They are the most accessible to an observer, similar to how the outermost skin of an onion is easy to touch and see.

Deeper into the onion, we find layers embodying the beliefs, norms and attitudes prevalent in that culture. It's less tangible, often requiring more insightful observation to understand, akin to the layers of the onion that are now becoming less apparent and more intrinsic to its core.

At the heart of the onion, embodying the core of our cultural analogy, lie the deep-seated cultural assumptions and values. Being the most concealed layer, these aspects are challenging to discern and comprehend, yet they form the foundational layer upon which all the other layers are built. They're the essence of the onion, the heart that gives it its distinct flavour and character.

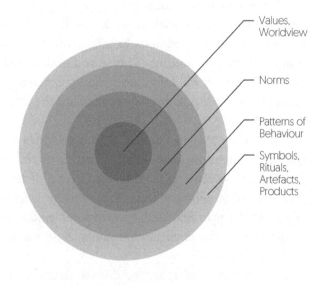

THE ONION MODEL

Therefore, an understanding of these layers and the dynamics of how they intermingle and influence each other are imperative. It's like how a chef needs to understand an onion's texture, flavour, and how it interacts with other ingredients to create a well-balanced dish.

3. Cultural Glasses Model: Perceiving the World Through Lenses

Have you ever thrown on a pair of neon-tinted sunglasses at a rock concert and suddenly found yourself in a world dripping in psychedelic colours? Welcome to Franz Boas's world – only his shades are a little more complex. Franz Boas, often dubbed the "Indiana Jones of Anthropology," reshaped our understanding of cultures in a way that was radical, daring and, let's be honest, pretty darn cool.

In the late 19th century, most Western thinkers strutted around confidently claiming that European culture was the 'headliner' of civilization's rock festival. Everyone else? Merely opening acts or, worse, just there for the backstage snacks. Along comes Boas, with his adventurous spirit, flipping the script to those naysayers.

After hanging out with the Inuit in the chilly terrains of Baffin Island and partying with the Kwakiutl tribes of the Pacific Northwest, Boas had an epiphany. It's as if he'd donned a pair of magic sunglasses — which he coined 'cultural glasses' — that let him see the world in its vibrant, diverse, chaotic glory. Every culture, Boas realized, has its own set of these groovy shades, colouring the world in unique hues and patterns. Boas made us see that our own cultures give us a particular playlist to groove to, a signature dance move, and a way to see the world that's all our own.

Why does this matter, especially in today's global jukebox of cultures? Every time we meet someone from another part of the world, we're not just having a chat – it's like a jam session with tunes from entirely different genres. Sometimes the music meshes, and we get jazz-fusion magic. Other times? It's a screechy remix that needs some tuning. But if we recognize we're all wearing our own snazzy 'cultural glasses,' the dance floor becomes a whole lot more harmonious.

Boas's rebellious idea was not just for kicks and giggles. At a time when colonialism was the head-banging metal of geopolitics, Boas was the soothing soul music preaching love, understanding and respect. His message was clear: No culture's sunglasses are cooler than another's; they're just different.

So, the next time you bump into someone and can't quite figure out their rhythm, remember Franz Boas and his funky cultural glasses. Remember that we are all culturally biased, as we are wearing our own cultural glasses without realizing that we are wearing them.

LANGUAGE AS A CULTURAL PRODUCT

Each time we wield the power of language or convey a message, we navigate cultural choices. Choosing language without understanding its cultural implications can lead to miscommunication and misunderstanding. Conversely, when conversing with someone who shares our language but not our cultural literacy, the words may be understood, but the meaning may be lost. Take, for example, the common American or British English greeting, "How are you?" In reality, it serves more as a "hello" than a genuine inquiry. A foreigner unfamiliar with this cultural nuance might interpret the question differently and offer a detailed response, only to find the asker seemingly disinterested. Alternatively, they might perceive the question as overly personal and inappropriate for a stranger. All languages have such social questions that appear as inquiries but serve more as greetings or icebreakers. In China and East Asia, "Where are you going?" and "Have you eaten?" exemplify this phenomenon. To an American, these questions might seem intrusive, but in their native context, no answer is truly expected.

As we have seen, anthropologist Franz Boas laid the foundations for cultural relativity, positing that individuals perceive the world within the confines of their own cultures. Anthropology's role, he believed, was to explore how culture shapes people and their interactions with the world. Boas advocated for examining the implications of culture and language to grasp these mechanisms, paving the way for the linguistic determinism hypothesis proposed by Eric Safir and Benjamin Lee Whorf. This hypothesis suggests that thought springs forth only through language, with concepts believed to exist from infancy fading away as language is learned.

Today, we see echoes of this hypothesis in various theories, including the linguistic relativity hypothesis, which suggests that language differences stem from both their linguistic structures and vocabulary. This hypothesis asserts that the language we speak alters our perception of the world and molds our concepts. People who speak different languages, it argues, possess distinct worldviews. For example, Russian and Greek speakers can more easily and swiftly differentiate shades of green and blue, as their languages identify these hues in greater detail. Another striking example can be found in languages that assign gender to objects, such as Spanish, French and German. Intriguingly, an object considered feminine in one language may be masculine in another. This seemingly random phenomenon affects how speakers of these languages process information, even when tested in their second languages. The essential takeaway is that language influences cognition and understanding, even when the language in question is not the speaker's native tongue.

Language, however, is not merely a reflection of culture, it is also a dynamic force that shapes and influences culture itself. Language provides a means of expressing and reinforcing cultural values and identities, and it can also be used to control and manipulate social behaviour. For example, language can be used to express cultural identity and to distinguish one group from another. Different dialects, accents and vocabulary choices can signal a person's regional or ethnic background and can create a sense of belonging to a particular cultural group.

Consider our naming conventions. My name starts with my family name, followed by my given name, and finally, my professional title, 'Xiang Catherine Dr.' This sequence is the exact inverse of the typical English naming convention. This serves as a straightforward yet profound example of the emphasis on group identity and lineage in Chinese culture. Despite having a population of 1.3 billion, only 100 surnames are commonly found in China. When Chinese individuals encounter my surname, they can trace it back to 项羽 (Xiàngyǔ), the Hegemon-King of the Western Chu State from 200 BC. In contrast, in the UK, a relatively smaller nation, there are more than 200,000 distinct surnames. The Western convention underscores individual identity; one's given name is often the initial piece of information shared during introductions.

My given name in Chinese is 骅 (Huá), containing the Chinese character for 'horse' (马) as a radical. This is no accident, as I was born in the Chinese zodiac year of the horse. My name, in essence, signifies a breed of magnificent horse – a metaphor encapsulating my parents' hopes for me to excel in life. In fact, it's not uncommon for those born in the year of the horse in China to have names with similar 'horse' radicals. You can see how just our names can provide insights into our cultural heritage and identity.

Idiomatic expressions and proverbs often carry cultural values, wisdom and beliefs that are passed down through generations. These linguistic elements can provide insights into a culture's priorities, values and worldview. For example, the English idiom "time is money" reflects the value of efficiency and productivity in Western cultures, while the Chinese proverb "家和万事兴" (jiā hé wàn shì xīng), which translates to "family harmony brings prosperity to everything," emphasizes the importance of family harmony in Chinese culture.

Remember, language is a cultural product because it is created and shaped by culture. It reflects the beliefs, values and customs of a particular society, and it is used as a means of communication among members of that society. In other words, language is the product of the representation of culture. At the same time, language also shapes and influences the culture as our society changes and evolves with time.

DIFFERENT COMMUNICATION STYLES ACROSS THE WORLD

Communication styles vary profoundly across cultures, melded by factors such as values, norms, social structures and historical experiences. These differences can be observed in verbal, nonverbal, written and graphic forms. Let's now look at the various aspects of verbal and nonverbal communication.

VERBAL COMMUNICATION

In the following passages, we'll unveil some critical dimensions along which communication styles can diverge across cultures. I also invite you to reflect on your own communication styles based on these dimensions, to gain a deeper understanding of how you wish to communicate with others. To achieve success in communicating with other cultures, it all begins with knowing yourself.

High-context vs. Low-context

Edward T. Hall's groundbreaking work unveiled the concepts of high-context and low-context cultures, providing the cornerstone for further exploration into the fascinating realm of diverse communication styles. In high-context cultures, much of the meaning in communication stems from the context, including nonverbal cues, shared knowledge and established relationships. Examples of high-context cultures encompass Japan, China and many Arab countries. On the other hand, low-context cultures, such as the United States and Germany, derive meaning more explicitly and rely heavily on the words themselves. In such cultures, communication tends to be more direct and precise.

Picture a business meeting, where a Japanese team (high-context culture) and an American team (low-context culture) come together. Let us observe how the high-context communication style unfolds.

During the meeting, the American team presents a proposal for a new project. They anticipate a clear response from the Japanese team, either in agreement or dissent. However, instead of providing a direct answer, the Japanese team leader responds with a tale of a past project that faced similar challenges, subtly hinting at potential issues that may arise if they proceed with the proposed project.

In this high-context communication style, the Japanese team leader does not directly express their concerns or disagreement with the proposal. Instead, they rely on the shared understanding of past experiences and the context provided by the story to convey their message. The Japanese team trusts that the American team will pick up on these indirect cues and comprehend the underlying concerns.

In contrast, the American team, hailing from a low-context culture, might struggle to grasp the message conveyed by the Japanese team leader, as they are more accustomed to direct and explicit communication. This disparity in communication styles can lead to misunderstandings or confusion between the two teams if they are not aware of the cultural differences in their communication preferences.

The differences in communication can also impact relationship-building in business. A high-context culture, such as French culture, could spend a significant amount of time building rapport in business negotiation, discussing topics such as culture, history and personal interests. They also frequently use indirect language and nonverbal cues to convey their messages, such as using humour and anecdotes to establish trust and create a friendly atmosphere. This may not suit a low-context culture such as Swedish. A Swedish team tends to be more focused on the specifics of the deal, using direct language and clear proposals to ensure that both parties are satisfied with the terms of the agreement. They may view the French team's focus on building a relationship as unnecessary or distracting from the task at hand. As a result, the French team may feel that the Swedish team is being overly transactional and not taking the time to build a relationship, while the Swedish team may feel that the French team is being vague or not getting to the point.

In summary, high-context communication extracts meaning from contextual cues, shared cultural norms and nonverbal signals, rather than depending solely on explicit verbal communication. Recognizing and adapting to this communication style is vital when interacting with high-context cultures to ensure effective communication and circumvent misunderstandings.

Directness vs. Indirectness

In the grand tapestry of human communication, we find ourselves woven into a complex pattern of expression, where thoughts and opinions take on different hues and textures depending on the culture. In Western lands like the United States and Germany, direct communication paints a vivid picture, valuing honesty and clarity above all else. Meanwhile, in the East, where Japan and China flourish, indirect communication weaves its intricate patterns, prioritizing harmony and face-saving by using the subtle threads of hints, metaphors and implications.

The artistry of indirectness finds its roots in contrasting techniques. In the West, the brushstrokes of grammar define its essence, employing longer structures and the subtleties of the subjunctive and conditional moods. In the East, the mastery lies in the speaker's approach, skirting around verbalization and shrouding intent in layers of nuance.

It's important to note that even within seemingly similar cultures, nuances abound. Directness is not uniform across Western societies, with varying degrees of subtlety present throughout Europe. For instance, English cultural norms are considered less direct than those of their European neighbours. Wierzbicka (1991) noted that English speakers favour 'indirectness' when it comes to acts aimed at eliciting a response, such as making a request or asking for help. In contrast, House and Kasper (1981) found that German speakers, along with Polish, Russian, Serbo-Croatian and Spanish, are more direct than their English counterparts when it comes to complaints and requests.

In a study conducted by House and Kasper, participants were asked to express their grievances with a flatmate who had worn a shirt without permission and left a stain. The German participants were more direct, stating the offence outright, while the English participants hinted at the wrongdoing. The English approach, as evidenced by phrases like "Terrible, this stain won't come off" or "Did you wear my shirt by any chance?" was decidedly less direct than the Germans, who might say, "You shouldn't have taken my shirt without asking my permission" or "You have ruined my shirt."

Of course, individuals also adjust their level of directness subject to the context, such as who they are speaking to, the nature of the matter in discussion, etc. Nonetheless, it is useful to keep in mind that you might be too direct for some and too vague for others to understand in an intercultural communication context. Be observant and notice how your level of directness alters in your daily life. More importantly, observe how your colleagues from different cultures communicate. Do you find that they communicate on the direct or indirect end of the spectrum compared to you?

Expressiveness vs. Restraint

In the dance of human interaction, the rhythm of emotional expression can vary as widely as the melodies of language itself. In the sun-kissed lands of the Mediterranean, where Italy and Spain hold court, emotions spill forth like fountains of passion, articulated through animated gestures, expressive faces, and the rise and fall of vocal intonations. But in the quietude of more restrained cultures like Finland or Japan, emotions are guarded treasures, held close to the chest and communicated through controlled, subtle exchanges. The students of China, when introduced to the exuberance of other cultures, may marvel at the flamboyant ballet of Italian hand gestures, pondering whether the old adage holds true: "If you tied the hands of an Italian, they wouldn't be able to speak."

Asian communication styles often favour a delicate balance between global and local goals, an interplay that leads to less assertive and expressive interactions. Within these intricate cultural tapestries, the response to a question may prioritize harmony and grace over the blunt hammer of fact, particularly when the truth might prove unpalatable or humiliating. Smutkupt and Barna (1976) remind us that in Thailand, for example, the voicing of doubts is a rare occurrence, especially when addressing one's elders or those of higher status.

As emotions are restrained, Asian cultures demonstrate a preference for self-control, eschewing grand declarations in favour of more moderate expressions. "Good" takes the place of "fantastic," and "not very good" softens the blow of "terrible." According to Gudykunst and Kim (1984), in such cultures, the sincerity of direct verbal expressions of love and respect may be cast under a cloud of suspicion. Even compliments and praise, when excessive, can provoke embarrassment rather than appreciation.

In stark contrast, Italian, Slavic and Jewish cultures, as well as American Black culture, revel in the effervescence of emotional expression. Whether sentiments are jubilant or sorrowful, these cultures value uninhibited emotional release, a celebration of the full spectrum of human feeling.

Though Arabic cultures share similarities with their high-context Asian counterparts, they too embrace the art of emotional expressiveness. The expressive nature of the Arabic language is showcased in its rich and varied vocabulary, offering a cornucopia of synonyms and evocative phrases that empower speakers to convey their thoughts with precision and nuance. This linguistic virtuosity is epitomized in Arabic poetry, where metaphor, simile and other literary devices paint vivid emotional landscapes.

As Zaharna (1995) argues, the assertiveness and expressiveness of Arabic culture reflect a preference for affect over accuracy, image over meaning, and form over function. In contrast, Asian cultures achieve the same ends through opposite means. Barnlund's (1975) study comparing the nonverbal communication patterns of Japanese and American participants in a communication game called "The Silent Game" revealed that Japanese culture values regulated, coordinated and conformist behaviour, while American culture prizes individualism, self-expression and deviation from the norm.

Isn't it amazing to see how different languages function as vital threads in different cultures? Different languages offer us a wide range of rhythms and steps.

Clarity vs. Ambiguity

Ambiguity is a dominant feature in the mysterious world of Asian communication, its presence woven into the core structures of languages like Japanese, Korean and Chinese. This inherent ambiguity enhances the allure of the utterance, requiring the listener to unravel the mystery through shared knowledge and context. As a result of low assertiveness and expressiveness, Asians tend to demonstrate higher ambiguity. In Japanese and Korean languages, verbs come at the end of sentence; in Chinese, subjects or objects come at the end of the sentence, which means that the illocutionary act of a sentence cannot be determined until the whole sentence has been uttered. In addition, ellipses and incomplete sentences are abundant in Chinese language. All such linguistic structures and features enhance the ambiguity of the utterance. Here's an example of ambiguity in Chinese:

Original Chinese sentence: "你去吗?" (Nǐ qù ma)
Literal translation: "You go?"

In this example, the Chinese sentence "你去吗?" is an incomplete sentence with an ellipsis. The context and the subject of the conversation are not provided in the sentence, so the listener needs to rely on the shared knowledge and context of the conversation to understand the meaning behind the question. Depending on the context, the sentence could be interpreted in various ways:

- Are you going to the party?
- Are you going to the meeting?
- Are you going to the store?

The ambiguity in Chinese due to ellipses and incomplete sentences allows for a concise and context-dependent communication style. But this beauty of enigma, so cherished in high-context cultures, can sow seeds of confusion and misunderstanding when speakers from low-context cultures seek to decipher the veiled messages, craving explicit information and clarity to grasp the intended meaning.

Ambiguity in Chinese language can also be found in idiomatic expressions, proverbs and indirect communication. Consider "成语" (chéngyǔ), traditional four-character idioms that encapsulate complex ideas and rich historical narratives in a concise form. These chengyu are often employed in conversation, their meaning reliant on the listener's knowledge of the story and cultural context.

For example, the idiom "塞翁失马" (Sài Wēng Shī Mǎ), which translates to "Old man from the frontier loses a horse," alludes to a tale in which an old man's lost horse returns with another horse in tow. The subsequent chain of events – the old man's son breaking his leg while riding the new horse, thereby sparing him from conscription – imparts the wisdom that blessings and misfortunes can be intertwined, and that it is difficult to predict the ultimate outcome of a given situation. Chinese speakers may invoke this idiom to comment on the uncertainty of a situation or the potential hidden benefits of a seemingly negative event.

The use of ambiguous expressions like 成语 (chéngyǔ) in Chinese culture allows speakers to communicate complex ideas and emotions in an indirect and concise manner, a reflection of the high-context nature of Chinese communication. To fully appreciate and interpret how ambiguity works, one must be steeped in the shared cultural background and context, understanding the unspoken cues that guide the choreography of human connection.

In addition to the inherent nature of the language differences, different cultures associate clarity and ambiguity with conversational convention and politeness differently. Clarity has been key in Western communication. Both Western linguists Grice (1975) and Lakoff (1978) consider clarity to be essential as the foundation of communicative competence and politeness. Whereas indirectness and vagueness are a very effective strategy of 'saving face' in the East for social harmony. This is particularly the case when it comes to rejection and criticism.

Formality vs. Informality

Formality is like the grand ball of communication, where participants dress up in their finest linguistic attire, adhering to strict etiquette and customs. As if attending a royal event, people take their roles seriously, paying close attention to their partners' positions, the setting and the occasion. This elegant dance reflects a society's values and respect for hierarchy, harmony and tradition. Much like the twists and turns of a gripping novel, the formal discourse is a structured, layered and intricate journey through words, where every pause, every inflection and every carefully chosen phrase plays a part in the unfolding drama.

On the other hand, informality is the friendly gathering of communication, a vibrant scene reminiscent of a lively book club discussion or a cosy fireside chat. There is warmth, familiarity and ease among participants, who feel comfortable enough to let down their guard and be their genuine selves. Laughter, casual banter and colloquial language colour the conversation, like the vivid and relatable characters in a best-selling book. In the realm of informality, the narrative is more spontaneous, and the plot is driven by authentic human connections.

Just as bestselling books captivate us with their engaging narratives, the difference between formality and informality invites us to embrace the nuances of communication and appreciate the unique qualities that make each culture and interaction a memorable tale worth experiencing.

Formality in communication varies across cultures, and understanding these differences is vital to establishing successful intercultural relationships. In countries like Australia and the United States, communication tends to be more informal, and people may address each other by their first names even in professional settings. This informality can create a relaxed atmosphere and help build rapport quickly. However, it may be perceived as disrespectful or inappropriate in cultures where formality is highly valued.

Conversely, in cultures where formality is the norm, such as South Korea, Japan and China, using titles and honorifics is crucial to show respect and maintain social harmony. In these cultures, adhering to established protocols, titles and conventions is vital, especially when addressing someone with a higher social status or authority.

For instance, in Japan, there are various honorific titles used to address someone, depending on their relationship and social status. Some common titles include "san" (さん) for general use, "sama" (様) for showing deep respect, "kun" (君) for addressing male friends or subordinates, and "chan" (ちゃん) for addressing children or close friends. Failing to use the appropriate title can be considered impolite or offensive.

In Chinese business culture, the use of formal titles in a workplace or formal setting is crucial. For instance, in a corporate environment, employees would address their manager with the title "经理" (jīnglǐ) and a company director with "董事" (dǒngshì). It is considered disrespectful to use someone's first name without their proper title, as it might lead to misunderstandings or harm professional relationships. This practice reflects the cultural importance of respect and hierarchy in professional interactions in China. In contexts where a choice is available, it is customary to opt for the higher title as a sign of respect. For instance, in Chinese, "院长" (yuàn zhǎng), meaning Dean, is preferred over "老师" (lǎoshī), meaning Teacher, even though a dean is also a teacher. This preference for higher titles reflects a cultural emphasis on hierarchy and respect. Additionally, the term 'deputy' is often omitted from titles to confer greater esteem.

This practice underscores the importance placed on status and respect in professional and social interactions.

NONVERBAL COMMUNICATION

Much of our communication is done via body language, facial expressions, gestures and eye contact. Research has shown that our communication is achieved 30% by what we say and 70% by how we say it.

Luckily, we share many expressions. This is how we can understand basic human emotions. Ekman and Friesen's groundbreaking 1971 study, "Constants across Cultures in the Face and Emotion," identified that facial expressions corresponding to six basic emotions – happiness, sadness, anger, fear, surprise and disgust – are universally recognized, regardless of one's cultural background. From the bustling cities of the United States and Japan to the remote Fore people of New Guinea, a smile means happiness and an angry face signifies anger.

But the story doesn't end there. Cultural factors can influence the intensity of emotional expressions and perceptions. Some cultures may openly display emotions, while others keep them under wraps. Just think of how Japanese participants might perceive anger as less intense than their American counterparts due to cultural norms. Knapp and Hall, in their eighth edition of *Nonverbal Communication in Human Interaction* (2013), describe the diverse landscape of nonverbal communication across cultures, ranging from personal space, eye contact, gestures and touch.

Picture yourself in a bustling American city, maintaining eye contact with a friend during a conversation. Suddenly, you're transported to a Japanese office, where avoiding direct eye contact with a superior is a sign of respect. The norms around gestures and touch can be just as diverse, with a friendly pat on the back being acceptable in the United States but frowned upon in Japan or Finland. Or perhaps, if British, you are feeling uneasy when a Brazilian or Saudi Arabian counterpart stands too close during a conversation. Each interaction can be delicate, where missteps can lead to misunderstandings.

Cultural differences in nonverbal communication can have significant implications for business interactions in an increasingly globalized world. Failing to recognize and adapt to these differences may lead to misunderstandings, damaged relationships and even lost opportunities. Let's have a look at some of the key implications for business.

Building relationships and trust

Nonverbal communication plays a vital role in establishing rapport and trust with business partners and clients. Being aware of cultural differences in gestures, facial expressions and body language can help create a positive first impression and foster strong professional relationships. When Walmart entered the German market, the company's practice of having greeters at store entrances and encouraging employees to smile at customers backfired. In German culture, smiling at strangers is less common and can be considered insincere or intrusive. As a result, Walmart struggled to build trust with German customers, ultimately leading to the company's exit from the German market in 2006, according to The Global Millennial (https://medium.com/). This case illustrates the importance of understanding cultural differences in nonverbal communication, such as smiling and greeting behaviours, to build trust and rapport with customers.

Negotiations and decision-making

In negotiations, understanding cultural variations in nonverbal cues can provide insights into the preferences, emotions and intentions of business partners. Subtle facial expressions or gestures may indicate satisfaction, disagreement or uncertainty, impacting the negotiation process and out-comes. People from some cultures, such as East Asia, are more likely to pay greater attention to such details, some-thing children are taught to do from a young age.

It's crucial to be mindful of how common gestures carry different meanings across cultures. Take, for instance, the American gesture for "OK," formed by a circle of the thumb and index finger. In France, this could imply 'nothing,' while in Japan, it's a symbol for money, and in Brazil, it's even con-sidered vulgar. Similarly, the familiar 'V for victory' sign, often seen as positive, is offensive in many European contexts.

Then there's the ubiquitous nodding of the head, commonly understood as agreement or affirmation in many places. Yet, in countries like China and Japan, this simple gesture might only indicate that the speaker is being heard, without any agree-ment implied. In Bulgaria, the plot thickens – a nod actually means 'no' and a side-to-side shake signifies 'yes.'

Conflict resolution

Misinterpretation of nonverbal cues may contribute to misunderstandings and conflicts in business settings. Being aware of cultural differences can help prevent conflicts and facilitate smoother conflict resolution. In the 1990s, Nike faced criticism over labour conditions in its Indonesian fac-tories. One of the key issues was the use of physical contact by factory managers to discipline workers, which was consid-ered acceptable by local cultural norms. However, the prac-tice was seen as a violation of workers' rights from a Western perspective. Nike was forced to address this issue and adapt its management practices to be more culturally sensitive.

Effective presentations and meetings

In business presentations and meetings, nonverbal com-munication influences audience engagement, receptive-ness and comprehension. Adapting nonverbal cues, such as eye contact, gestures and proximity, to suit the cultural context can ensure that messages are conveyed effectively and professionally. For example, in terms of interpersonal space and physical contact, cultural norms vary significantly. In the United States, heterosexual men generally avoid holding hands or touching each other, but this is not the case in many parts of Africa and the Middle East, where such actions are considered normal.

Your audience picks up nonverbal cues more than you might think. Slouching might suggest tiredness or lack of interest. Hands in pockets during business presentations could be interpreted as boredom or a lack of professionalism. Standing upright often signals excitement, confidence and interest. Leaning toward someone during a conversation can indicate keen interest or the perceived importance of what's being said. Your posture, whether standing in a conference room or sitting at your desk, continuously conveys your emotional state.

Team collaboration

Business teams often comprise members from various cultural backgrounds, making it essential to understand and respect differences in nonverbal communication. This understanding can promote effective collaboration, create a more inclusive work environment, and prevent misinterpretations or discomfort among team members.

During the development of the Airbus A380, a large-scale collaboration between European countries, miscommunication between the French and German teams led to significant delays and cost overruns, according to *Financial Times*. One contributing factor was the different cultural expectations regarding nonverbal communication, which led to misunderstandings and tension. French engineers considered direct eye contact a sign of honesty and trust, while their German counterparts viewed it as confrontational.

International business etiquette

Adhering to culturally appropriate norms in areas such as personal space, touch and greetings can create a favourable impression and enhance cross-cultural business relationships. Simple things such as presenting one's business card or gifts with both hands are considered polite and proper in Chinese and Japanese cultures.

Virtual communication

With the rise of remote work and virtual meetings, interpreting nonverbal cues accurately has become more challenging. Communication via video calls creates the closest form of synchronous computer-mediated communication (CMC) to face-to-face interaction.

By becoming attuned to the nuances of nonverbal communication across different cultures, you enhance your ability to engage effectively across international and virtual settings. Notice how nonverbal cues might vary between individuals you know well and those you don't, as well as between those from your own culture and those from different cultural backgrounds. This practice can be both enlightening and enjoyable, offering a deeper understanding of the unspoken languages that permeate our interactions. Embrace it as a fun and educational journey!

SUMMARY

To navigate the vast terrains of cultural intricacies, we have rooted our understanding in three foundational pillars: the clarity provided by cultural models, the profound influence of culture on language use, and the myriad communication styles that form the world's conversational landscape.

Cultural models act as our compass, presenting frameworks that shine a light on the unseen threads binding societies together. By identifying these patterns, we are better equipped to appreciate the vast array of human experiences and values.

Language is more than just a medium for communication; it stands out as a formidable shaper of thought. It mirrors deeper societal subtleties, serving both as a gateway into cultures and as a prism through which communities perceive the world.

Furthermore, delving into communication styles emphasizes that there isn't a universal manner of articulating thoughts or emotions. Celebrating this diversity lays the foundation for richer, more compassionate interactions, even when they push us beyond our cultural comfort zones.

As we conclude this foundational chapter, it becomes clear that grasping these basics is akin to possessing a key – one that unveils avenues to deeper empathy, expansive perspectives and more purposeful engagements in our global community. With these insights, we become more than just observers of culture; we are active participants, poised to engage with the world's vibrant mosaic of traditions, beliefs and communicative intricacies.

CHAPTER 2

The Chinese Language

At the heart of East Asia lies a linguistic gem that has evolved, influenced and resonated for millennia: the Chinese language. With its poetic nuances, intricate characters and vast array of dialects, Chinese language offers valuable insights into China's history, culture and philosophy. To appreciate the depth and breadth of Chinese, it's essential to explore its multifaceted dimensions. This chapter will guide you through the mesmerizing maze of Chinese characters' development, its unique writing system, the widely-spoken Mandarin Chinese, and the colourful spectrum of other dialects that breathe life into China.

FIRST THINGS FIRST –
DEMYSTIFYING LEARNING CHINESE

Imagine this: you're familiar only with common European languages and suddenly, you stumble upon the rich tapestry of the Chinese language. It's like nothing you've ever seen before. Yet, it commands the attention of more speakers globally than any other language. Not to mention, it houses the world's oldest literature, a magnificent library that stretches back a whopping 35 centuries. In English, there is a saying: "It's all Greek to me!" And guess what Greeks say? "It's all Chinese to me!"

To a Western observer, the Chinese writing system appears almost like a secret code. Instead of neat rows of straightforward alphabetic letters, Chinese offers thousands of distinctive characters, many beautifully complicated, captivating the eye like a piece of art. When heard, the language feels melodious, almost like a serene song filling your ears.

I don't blame you if you are under the impression that Chinese is impossible to learn. Chinese is a world apart from European languages, making understanding of its structure and historical evolution essential for anyone who is seeking a broad comprehension of the nature of human language.

And there are surprises when you dig a little deeper. The basic Chinese language structure is refreshingly uncomplicated, even simpler in many aspects compared to Western languages. There are 21 initials (and two special initials) and 38 finals in Chinese Pinyin. Some initials and some finals cannot be combined. According to certain rules, all these initials and finals can form a total of about 400 syllables, although pronunciation rules in English are far more complex than that.

Chinese language eschews verb conjugations and noun declensions. The tedious paradigms that make Western schoolchildren groan in their grammar lessons? You won't find them in a Chinese grammar book. For example, the verb 'to buy' manifests in English as 'buy,' 'buys,' 'bought,' and 'buying.' In Chinese, it's simply '买.' The context mostly clarifies what tense, mood, number or case is intended, making the language practically free of what many might see as redundancy in its grammar. And there are no genders or cases.

The Chinese writing system is separate from spoken language. In other words, you can learn to speak Mandarin without having to read and write Chinese characters. On the other hand, you can fully comprehend Chinese without knowing how to say it. It is perfectly possible to reach a conversational level in Mandarin within six months. Only when you wish to learn the language systemically does it require time and greater effort.

One of the key differences between Chinese and other European languages is that Chinese characters determine the pronunciation and meaning, not the other way around. In other words, each Chinese character is a combination of three elements: the shape/writing of the character, the pronunciation and the meaning.

During the London School of Economics (LSE) graduation season, I'm often presented with a list of Chinese names, transliterated into Western spelling by our ceremony office. They seek assistance in providing a pronunciation guide. They are astonished when I tell them that I can't provide the pronunciation without seeing the Chinese characters or having the tone markers above the spelling. This is rooted in the unique nature of Chinese, where each character can have up to four different pronunciations. The prevalent misconception is that spelling directly correlates to meaning. While this is sometimes true in Chinese, it isn't always the case. A single phonetic sound can correspond to over 10 distinct Chinese characters. Thus, sound alone is insufficient.

At one point in Chinese history, some people argued to simply replace the difficult Chinese character written system with Romanized spelling system. The esteemed Chinese linguist Zhao Yuanren (赵元任, 1892–1982), the pioneer Chinese teacher at Harvard, eloquently argued for the importance of retaining Chinese characters. He crafted a renowned poem titled "The Lion-Eating Poet in the Stone Den" (施氏食狮史) in the 1930s. In this poem, a total of just over 90 characters are utilized, yet they all share the phonetic sound — 'shi,' albeit with varied tones.

While many are aware that Chinese is a tonal language, this poem exemplifies its intricacy to the extreme. Reading it aloud without the Chinese characters can bewilder even native speakers, but they can understand the poem once seeing the Chinese characters. This is because each character is associated with a different core meaning. Zhao's principal argument focused on the pivotal role characters play: even if one speaks the language fluently, without recognizing Chinese characters, communication barriers arise.

THE SPOKEN LANGUAGE
MANDARIN CHINESE

Standard Mandarin, known in China as 普通话 (Pǔtōng-huà), meaning 'common speech,' is the most widely spoken language in the world. It serves as China's official language, the lingua franca that bridges the vast regional and cultural diversity of the country's 1.3 billion inhabitants. It is also spoken in Hong Kong, Taiwan, Singapore and Malaysia.

This language, based on the Beijing dialect (native to about 830 million Chinese), is now taught throughout China, offering a sound structure that is surprisingly straightforward – often simpler than the straightforward syllables of languages like Spanish. However, it does present one intriguing element that may seem alien to speakers of European languages: tonal inflection.

The unique melodic rhythm that gives Chinese its distinctive sound comes from this tonal nature. Nearly every syllable in Standard Chinese is expressed in one of four fundamental tones. These tones are represented visually in Pinyin through diacritical marks placed above the vowels.

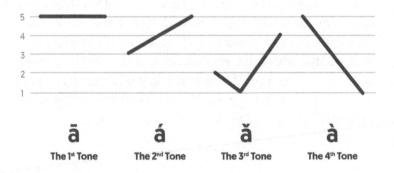

FOUR TONES IN CHINESE

You might think of this tonal feature as a musical score, a dimension primarily found in Chinese and a handful of Southeast Asian languages influenced by it. In essence, each Chinese syllable dances to a distinct pitch pattern or 'tone.' Modifying the tone can change the meaning of a syllable as dramatically as altering a consonant or vowel does in English.

Let's consider the English name 'John.' We use a rising pitch pattern to ask, "John?" and a falling pitch pattern to exclaim, "John!" These varied tones convey different emotions, but 'John' remains 'John.' In contrast, in Chinese, the syllable "ma" with a rising tone could mean "hemp," while "ma" with a falling tone could signify "to scold." The meanings of these tonally distinct syllables are as unrelated as the English words "me" and "mad." Below is a summary of the four tones in Mandarin Chinese with examples:

First Tone (ˉ): High and level.
E.g., 妈 (mā) "mother"

Second Tone (´): Rising, like a questioning intonation in English.
E.g., 麻 (má) "hemp"

Third Tone (ˇ): Starts low, dips, then rises.
E.g., 马 (mǎ) "horse"

Fourth Tone (`): Sharp and falling.
E.g., 骂 (mà) "scold"

A slight change in tone transforms 'mā' (mother) into 'mǎ' (horse). The importance of mastering tones couldn't be clearer. You certainly wouldn't want to inadvertently call your mother a horse!

However, the spelling system you've observed didn't exist until the mid-20th century. Introduced in the 1950s by the

Chinese government, 拼音 (Pīnyīn), meaning 'spelled sounds' in English, served as a revolutionary bridge to cross the barrier between the Latin alphabet and Chinese characters.

Pinyin is a system of phonetic notation that uses the Latin alphabet to transcribe Mandarin sounds. Each Chinese character is assigned a Romanized equivalent, making it easier for learners to grasp pronunciation. For example, the Mandarin word for 'peace,' written in characters as '和平,' is transcribed as *hépíng* in *Pinyin*.

Pinyin also played a crucial role in increasing literacy rates in China in the 1950s and 1960s. Nowadays, it's widely used for typing Chinese characters on digital devices, making it a crucial component of contemporary communication.

The creation and adoption of *Pinyin* underscores the blend of tradition and innovation in the Chinese language, providing an accessible pathway into the world of Mandarin. It is testament to how language adapts over time, catering not only to cultural preservation but also to the practical needs of communication in an ever-evolving world.

Case Study:
Tonal Language and Evidence
from our Brain

Background: Mandarin is a tonal language. Changing the tone of a word can alter its meaning entirely, leading to humorous or even embarrassing mix-ups. Mispronouncing the tone can transform "Can I ask you something?" (我可以问你吗？) into "Can I kiss you?" (我可以吻你吗？). What is even more fascinating is that such differences are now captured in our brain scans.

The study: A ground-breaking study conducted at MIT in 2015 looked at the cross-language differences in brain networks responsible for intelligible speech. Utilizing cloud-computing and functional MRI dynamic causal modelling analysis, researchers compared over 4,000 models of cortical dynamics among critical language regions in the temporal and frontal cortex. They established bias-free information flow maps that were shared or specific for processing intelligible speech in Chinese (a tonal language) and English (a nontonal language). Furthermore, the study unveiled the neural dynamics between the left and right hemispheres during Chinese speech comprehension.

Key findings: Language processing is predominantly a left hemisphere activity. Both Chinese and English speakers have active information flow in the left hemisphere network of the brain. However, the study revealed that tonal speakers, such as those speaking Chinese, engage the right hemisphere more actively compared to nontonal English speakers. The lateral brain images display information flow between the left and right sides of the brain network, particularly to and from the R region of the right hemisphere.

Implications: This study demonstrates that interactions among the typical left hemispheric language regions differ across languages. For tonal language speakers, both the left and right hemispheric language regions must function successfully to comprehend intelligible speech. In other words, your brain must work harder to decode meaning. So, the next time you feel a headache coming on while learning Mandarin, don't be surprised. Instead, consider it a healthy sign that your brain is being trained.

The findings of this study are captivating, as they unveil the intricate relationship between our languages and the functioning of our brains. The physiological and neurological connection between languages and brain function is one aspect of a multifaceted cognitive landscape, shedding light on the incredible power of our minds as they navigate the world of language.

OTHER SPOKEN LANGUAGES

As we have seen, Mandarin is the most widely spoken language group in China, spoken by almost 70% of the population. Mandarin itself includes various regional sub-dialects, such as Northeastern Mandarin, Ji-Lu Mandarin, Jiao-Liao Mandarin and more.

China is home to a fascinating mosaic of dialects and languages, each imbued with its own unique history, characteristics and cultural nuances. These variants are not just 'accents' but can be vastly different in terms of vocabulary, syntax and pronunciation, so much so that they are often mutually unintelligible. Here's a brief introduction to some of other main dialect groups in China:

- **吴 (Wú, Shanghainese):** Wu is spoken in the Yangtze River Delta region, including the bustling city of Shanghai and parts of Jiangsu and Zhejiang provinces. This language group, with a high level of internal diversity, has over 70 million speakers.

- **粤 (Yuè, Cantonese):** Famous around the world due to the historical emigration from its region, Yue, or Cantonese, is spoken in Guangdong and Guangxi provinces, as well as Hong Kong and Macau. It is known for having a more complex tone system than Mandarin.

- **闽 (Mǐn):** Predominantly spoken in the Fujian province, Taiwan, and by Chinese communities in Southeast Asia, Min dialects are some of the most divergent and are split into several subgroups such as Min Bei, Min Dong, Min Zhong, Min Nan (which includes Hokkien and Teochew) and Puxian.

- **晋 (Jìn):** Spoken in Shanxi province and parts of Inner Mongolia, Jin was historically considered a part of Mandarin but has recently been recognized as its own group due to its distinctive features.

- **湘 (Xiāng, Hunanese):** Xiang is mainly spoken in Hunan province. It has been significantly influenced by Mandarin and is often divided into new and old Xiang, with the old variant containing more distinct features.

- **客家 (Kèjiā, Hakka):** Spoken by the Hakka people in several provinces across the country, Hakka has numerous local variants but maintains a level of mutual intelligibility.

- **平话 (Pínghuà):** This is spoken in parts of the Guangxi Zhuang Autonomous Region and has two major sub-dialects: Northern and Southern Pinghua.

- **徽 (Huī):** While spoken by fewer people and often overlooked, the Huizhou dialects have a significant historical impact and are known for their preservation of many ancient features.

While these represent the major dialects of Chinese, there are many more regional variants and sub-dialects that enrich the linguistic tapestry of the country. Understanding this diversity is crucial to appreciating China's rich cultural and linguistic heritage. So, don't be surprised if people from Hong Kong teach you something that sounds nothing like what your colleagues from Mainland China say.

CHINESE CHARACTERS AND WRITING SYSTEM

As one of the world's oldest continuously used writing sys-tems, Chinese characters, or 汉字 (Hànzì), offer a unique window into the deep historical and cultural legacy of one of the world's most ancient civilizations. Unlike Western languages with their alphabets, the Chinese language greets you with a vast sea of intricate and beautiful characters, each like a mesmerizing work of art.

There are nearly 57,000 characters in total. Knowledge of 2,500–3,000 characters is necessary for reading newspapers and most other common purposes. The characters you read in this book are the simplified script system, most of which contain fewer strokes per character. This system was made official in 1952 and is used in mainland China. In Taiwan and Hong Kong, people still use the traditional script system.

Immerse yourself in the ancient world of Chinese script, where the earliest writings emerge, not from ink on paper, but etched into bone and tortoise shell. The inscriptions, bearing prophetic messages regarding political, religious events, weather forecasts and battles, narrate tales from an era long past. Unearthed in the late 19th century from Chinese apothecaries, where they were traded as potent 'dragon bones,' the story of these inscriptions paints a vibrant picture in the annals of Chinese archaeology and philology. Today, over 100,000 such inscribed fragments have been discovered.

Throughout history, Chinese characters have found life on diverse mediums, such as metal vessels, stone drums, jade jewellery, coins, metal mirrors, and even bricks and tiles. However, the central evolution was the transition to the brush—used on silk, bamboo, wood and finally paper. Unlike a rigid stylus, the brush's fluidity offers variations in thick-ness, providing the artist with expansive creative liberty in character portrayal. This is now considered as an art form called Chinese calligraphy. It is very much appreciated in Japan as well. As a matter of fact, 30% of Japanese writing is in Chinese characters, which makes it easy for Chinese tourists to navigate Japan.

Another remarkable aspect of the Chinese writing system is the importance of strokes and stroke order. Writing a character involves following a precise sequence of brush strokes, a discipline that becomes a meditative act. It's no wonder that calligraphy holds such a high place in Chinese culture, considered akin to painting, with brushwork valued as much for its artistic as its communicative merit. Chinese calligraphy has various styles, which also represent the evolution of Chinese characters over time.

From the very beginning, Chinese characters have woven together the visual and the conceptual. The earliest known Chinese characters were inscriptions on oracle bones, dating back to the Shang dynasty in the second millennium BC. These characters were often pictorial representations of the words they stood for, turning the act of writing into an artistic endeavour. Take a look at the image to the right, showing the evolution of Chinese characters from the most ancient form to modern use. The character for 'mountain,' for instance, indeed resembles a mountain.

	oracle bone *jiaguwen*	greater seal *dazhuan*	lesser seal *xiaozhuan*	clerkly script *lishu*	standard script *kaishu*	running script *xingshu*	cursive script *caoshu*	modern simplified *jiantizi*
rén (*nin) human								
nǚ (*nraʔ) woman								
ěr (*nhaʔ) ear								
mǎ (*mrǎʔ) horse								
yú (*ŋha) fish								
shān (*srān) mountain								
rì (*nit) sun								
yuè (*ŋot) moon								
yǔ (*whaʔ) rain								
yún (*wan) cloud								

ANCIENT SCRIPTS OF THE WORLD

While many characters have evolved over time and no longer visually represent their meaning, this pictorial legacy remains an intrinsic part of the system. The way the ancient Chinese formed new characters reflects their values and beliefs. You might find it interesting to discover that the character for 'woman' next to the character for 'child' composes the character for 'good,' as it was considered beneficial for a woman to stay together with her child. Similarly, the character for 'woman' beneath the character for 'roof' signifies 'protection' or 'peace.' At that time, men could have several wives in the house and, as a result, one could only find peace with one woman at home. I highly recommend the book series *Fun with Chinese Characters* by Tan Huay Peng. I love the way the author presents the concepts to make them engaging.

Each character in the Chinese language can be a word on its own or combined with others to form compound words, adding another layer of complexity and intrigue. This interplay of symbols also contributes to the lyrical beauty of Chinese poetry and prose, which often relies on homophones and wordplay.

- **Compound Words:** This is the most common way words are formed in Chinese. Two or more characters, each with their own meaning, are combined to create a new word. For instance, the word for 'computer' in Chinese is '电脑' (diànnǎo), where '电' (diàn) means 'electricity' and '脑' (nǎo) means 'brain,' so 'electric brain' equates to 'computer.'

- **Associated Meaning:** Sometimes words are formed by combining two characters that relate to the concept of the new word. For instance, the word 'restaurant' is '餐厅' (cāntīng), where '餐' (cān) means 'meal' and '厅' (tīng) means 'hall.' When combined, they create the concept of a 'meal hall' or a 'restaurant.'

- **Antonyms or Contrastive Pairs:** Some Chinese words are formed by putting together two characters with opposite meanings. This is used to express an inclusive or general concept. For instance, '老小' (lǎoxiǎo), literally 'old small,' means 'everyone' from the oldest to the youngest. 'Buy' and 'sell' combine to form 'business' – '买卖' (mǎimài).

- **Synonyms or Reduplication:** In certain cases, characters with similar meanings are combined, or a character is simply repeated, to create a new word. For example, '学习' (xuéxí), where both '学' (xué) and '习' (xí) have the meaning of 'to learn.' The resulting term means 'to study.' Reduplication, such as '妈妈' (māma), meaning 'mother,' often results in terms that are more colloquial, casual or endearing.

Chinese vocabulary is deeply rooted in historical references and nuanced cultural connotations. Many terms extend beyond their literal translations, encapsulating layers of meaning that can easily be missed by those unfamiliar with the culture. Consider, for instance, the phrase '带绿帽子' (Dài lǜmàozi, literally 'to wear a green hat'). In Chinese culture, this implies that a man's wife is being unfaithful. The expression comes from a true historical story where a wife gives her husband a green hat whenever he travels away for days on business. She sells the idea to the husband that the bright colour will bring him more business, but in reality, the green hat serves as a signal to her lover, their neighbour, that he can visit since the husband is not around. Owing to this potent cultural association, it's rare for Chinese men to wear green hats. Moreover, presenting such an item as a gift to a Chinese friend could be considered a major blunder. Not understanding these linguistic subtleties can pose genuine challenges, especially in the realm of business. The case study below illustrates the point further.

Case study:
IKEA's Tofu Ice Cream
Controversy in Hong Kong

Introduction: Successful advertising often strives to connect with its audience using cultural references. However, such attempts can backfire when messages are misinterpreted or perceived as insensitive, as IKEA's 2019 advertisement for tofu ice cream in Hong Kong demonstrates.

The Event: In May 2019, IKEA unveiled an advertisement for their new tofu ice cream. While the promotion aimed to highlight the product's delectable taste, the tagline, "You can eat my tofu whenever you want," became a significant point of contention. In Cantonese slang, the phrase "eating someone's tofu" (食豆腐) is synonymous with making unwanted sexual advances.

Accompanied by the ad's pink aesthetics and a playful social media note – "You guys can eat [my tofu], but please be gentle" – the campaign was instantly mired in controversy.

Public Outcry: The feminist activist group Gender and Sexual Justice in Action was quick to call out the ad's perceived insensitivity. In a Facebook statement, they said, "[The ad] generates the image of a woman wishing for her body to be eaten like tofu ... The ice-cream ad once again treats women's bodies as objects to be taken advantage of [by men]."

This condemnation from the activist group triggered mixed reactions online. While many expressed outrage at IKEA's lack of cultural sensitivity, others felt that the feminist group was overanalysing a simple ice cream ad, accusing them of being overly sensitive.

IKEA's Response: In defence of its ad, IKEA responded by stating their intention was purely to communicate in a light-hearted manner, highlighting the creamy texture of the ice cream. They said, "The latest tofu-flavored sundae promotional post 'speaks' for itself to emphasize the silky taste."

Conclusion: Cultural nuances and sensitivities play a pivotal role in advertising. While attempting to resonate with audiences using colloquialisms and cultural references, brands must exercise caution. IKEA's tofu ice cream debacle underscores the need for thorough market research, cultural understanding and the importance of gauging public sentiment before launching any campaign.

Understanding how words are formed in Chinese can give language learners and enthusiasts valuable insight into the logic underlying the language, making it an intriguing and rewarding area of study. Moreover, being aware of the hidden cultural meaning of the words and stories behind the formation of the words can be useful and fun, not only for learners but also for international businesses.

SUMMARY

Chinese, with its 35-century-old literary legacy, often stands as an enigma, its script appearing as intricate artwork and its spoken form resembling a harmonious song. Yet, unlike the multifaceted verb forms and noun declensions in Western languages, Chinese streamlines its grammar, relying heavily on context.

While the structure of spoken Chinese, especially Mandarin, seems straightforward – with 21 initials, 38 finals and about 400 syllables – the Chinese writing system, separate from its spoken form, is where the complexity lies. Each character is a trinity: visual representation, pronunciation and meaning.

The Chinese language, with its multitude of characters and tonal nuances, stands as a testament to the power of human expression, inviting learners to immerse themselves in a cultural odyssey unlike any other.

CHAPTER 3

Chinese Thought Pattern

Now that we've explored different theorical models in understanding culture and had an introduction to Chinese language, it's time to arm ourselves with a foundational grasp of how thought processes are intertwined with language. Just as a botanist first understands the essence of plants before delving into the vast flora of a rainforest, our exploration of the Chinese thought paradigm requires an appreciation of certain core principles. This chapter will illuminate three central concepts that are indispensable: 1) How language reflects our thought processes; 2) How the East and West think differently; 3) Chinese thought patterns found in communication.

LANGUAGE AS A THOUGHT PROCESS SYSTEM

In an ancient land, Buddha once whispered a profound truth: "We are what we think. All that we are arises with our thoughts. With our thoughts, we make the world." While I stand in agreement with the wise sage, I propose a slight modification to his words: we are what we communicate. For without that little voice inside our heads, we cannot think. Our thoughts, expressed through the symphony of verbal and nonverbal communication, profoundly impact our thinking, behaviour and psyche.

Throughout history, scholars from diverse fields – linguists, philosophers, cognitive scientists, psychologists and anthropologists – have debated and investigated the relationship between language and thought. Language, a symbolic tool wielded by our minds, communicates our thoughts and represents our cognitive processes. In essence, language is the looking glass through which we perceive our thoughts and the world around us.

As the philosopher Wittgenstein mused, the boundaries of our language shape our world. It is through the words we speak and the languages we embrace that our thoughts find form and our perceptions diversify.

But what, you may ask, is a thought? Let's do a simple experiment. Close your eyes and imagine a ripe, red apple. Wait for 60 seconds before you open your eyes again. Now, tell me what has gone through your mind during that minute. As your eyes trace the curves of the apple skin, your mind may flood with words like 'delicious' or 'fresh' and phrases like, "An apple a day keeps the doctor away," flitting through your consciousness, prompting you to ponder whether it's time to replenish your fruit bowl. Then work matters float in ... the emails you need to reply and the report you've got to finish! Or perhaps you thought to yourself, "Is 60 seconds over? Can I open my eyes now? Hmmm, that's the longest 60 seconds ever!"

This is the essence of thought – a collection of words, stored in the depths of our minds, waiting to be summoned into existence. As we think, we traverse the web of associations and memories within our minds, each word leading to another until a new sensation or experience redirects our attention.

Many view language as a mere function of the body or a collection of words and sentences. But language is so much more – it is a mental process that shapes our thinking and our lives. Our thoughts are composed of words and sentences, woven together by the grammar and rules of language. In this way, language serves as both a system and a mental process that sculpts our perceptions and understanding. Language and thought are symbiotic entities; they begin their journey in parallel, only to intertwine further down the road, shaping each other in fascinating ways.

EAST AND WEST: HOW WE THINK DIFFERENTLY

Have you ever noticed how people from different parts of the world approach problems or see things differently? It's not just coincidence; it's deeply rooted in our cultural backgrounds.

Westerners often approach things in an analytical way. They love to get into the nitty-gritty, categorize items and dissect issues. It's like looking at individual trees in a forest.

Now, imagine looking at the same forest, but instead of focusing on individual trees, you see the entire area and how everything connects. That's more like the Eastern perspective, which emphasizes a holistic, connected viewpoint. It's about seeing the bigger picture and understanding the relationships within.

Researchers like Professor Richard Nisbett have delved deeply into these cultural thought differences. In his book *The Geography of Thought*, Professor Nisbett traces back Western analytical thinking to ancient Greece, where the focus was on categorizing and logic. In contrast, Eastern traditions like Taoism and Confucianism encourage a more holistic view, seeking a middle ground and emphasizing the interconnectedness of things.

Why these differences, though? Some experts believe it's due to the social complexities of ancient societies. For instance, ancient Chinese culture required individuals to maintain close ties and be sensitive to their community's nuances. In comparison, ancient Greece, being less socially complex, allowed for more individual focus.

There's some evidence that shows these differences in action. In one study, American children categorized objects based on what they were (birds or mammals, for example), while Chinese children grouped the same objects based on their relationships (a cat chases a mouse). Ji, Nisbett and Zhang (2001) found similar differences between Chinese and American undergraduates asked to group together two of three different words such as seagull, squirrel and grass. Chinese students were more likely to group on the basis of relationships (the squirrel runs on the grass) and American students were more likely to group on the basis of taxonomic categories (seagulls and squirrels are both animals).

This doesn't mean one way of thinking is superior to the other; they're simply different. Recognizing these differences can bridge gaps, leading to improved global collaboration and better business outcomes.

Case Study:
Nike's Cultural Misstep in
Celebrating Chinese New Year

Introduction: The global marketplace is rife with opportunities for brands to connect with diverse audiences. However, genuinely resonating with a culture requires more than just superficial knowledge. Nike's 2016 Chinese New Year shoe design serves as an illustrative example of the pitfalls of cultural marketing if not executed thoughtfully.

The Design: In an earnest attempt to celebrate Chinese New Year, Nike launched a series of shoes infused with symbolic Chinese elements. Their design featured two Chinese characters: '发,' denoting wealth or prosperity, and '福,' meaning good fortune. The company even used the colour red – synonymous with good luck in Chinese culture. Going a step further, they turned the '福' character upside down, mirroring a traditional Chinese practice signifying the arrival of good fortune.

The Oversight: The devil, as they say, is in the detail. When positioned side by side, the characters '发' and '福' combine to read '发福,' a term humorously referring to gaining weight or becoming fat. This unintentional message became the focal point for Chinese consumers.

Public Reaction: The message of unintentional weight gain on a shoe, especially during a festive period when people aspire for positivity, was far from ideal. The design was quickly ridiculed, turning Nike's Chinese New Year celebration shoes into a subject of jest across China.

Conclusion: Efforts to embrace cultural symbols can be commendable, but it's essential to ensure a holistic understanding and perspective. Nike's oversight in this campaign emphasises the importance of in-depth cultural research and validation. It's not enough to merely incorporate cultural elements; brands must understand how they interact and the broader messages they convey.

CHINESE THOUGHT PATTERNS AND WRITTEN COMMUNICATION

Differing thought patterns exert substantial influence on writing and translation, crafting unique styles and approaches that colour the world of language in vivid hues. Let's take a comparative approach. If we compare Chinese with English, you'll find English to be a fascinating hybrid – partially synthetic and partially analytical. Its overt grammar, hypostasis in syntax, relative freedom of word order, and flexible word formation act as its signature features. On the other hand, Chinese is more about the seamless flow of ideas and coherence over formality.

Let's take a closer look:

A. WORD ORDER

As Chinese culture is collective, it is fascinating to see this group mentality reflected in the language, particularly in the expression of time. In Chinese, time is expressed in the sequence of year, month, date, day, and time:

2023年4月6日，星期四上午9点
2023 year, 4 month, 6 day, Thursday, AM, 9 o'clock

This pattern is the exact opposite of English, which moves from specific to general.

Similarly, Chinese expressions of addresses follow this collective logic, beginning with the country, then city, town, and house number.

1. Country, Province Zipcode	Mr. John Williams **5**
	4 **3**
	6-305 Shao-Yuan Building
	Peking University **2**
2. Town/Area	Beijing, 100871 **1**
	People's Republic of China **1**
3. Building Name	

or

4. Floor, House Number	**1** 中国 北京 100871
	2 **3** **4**
	北京大学 绍园 6 号楼 305 房间
5. Individual or Businesss Name, Title	**5** 约翰·威廉姆斯 先生

WRITING OF ADDRESS IN ENGLISH AND CHINESE

This demonstrates the importance of collective information in the Chinese mindset. Chinese grammar rules for time and location also use the concept of the whole being more important than the individual parts. Once again, the sequence contrasts sharply with that of individualistic societies like the United Kingdom and the United States.

B. SENTENCE STRUCTURE

Chinese sentences are contextually driven, prioritizing coherence over formality. Sentence order unveils the inner logical relationship of the statement, while English sentences adhere to strict grammatical rules. Consider these examples:

"天气较好,我们去爬山" translates to "As the weather was fine, we decided to climb the mountain."

"与狗相比,猫更好一些" becomes "Cats are nicer than dogs."

However, if we look at the sentences themselves, they wouldn't be grammatically correct according to English grammar. Here is the direct translation following the Chinese sentence structure:

"天气较好,我们去爬山." = "Weather is better, we go climbing."

"与狗相比,猫更好一些." = "Compare to dogs, cats are better."

As we can see, it is not correct to construct sentences in the English language in the Chinese manner, yet it is perfectly possible in the Chinese language. The translation from Chinese to English requires restructuring the sentences to make them grammatically accurate in English.

C. TEXT ORGANIZATION

Chinese text often approaches a topic indirectly and follows a circular development pattern, while English tends to present the argument upfront and then dissects it. Scollon (2000:93) mentioned, "Western cultures use a deductive method of reasoning or argument, while Eastern culture uses an inductive method of reasoning."

Consider these two essays titled "An Early Morning Walk," one by a Chinese student and the other by a Western student, highlighting the different thought patterns.

Essay 1:
An Early Morning Walk
(Chinese Student)

In the stillness of dawn, as most souls remain ensconced in the warmth of their beds, the world outside awakens in a subtle ballet of nature. Birds begin their harmonious songs, dew-kissed leaves glisten in the first rays of sunlight, and the streets come alive with a serene energy. There's a tranquillity that's felt deeply when one immerses oneself in this symphony of the morning.

Stepping outside, the chill in the air is evident, caressing the face gently. Each step on the pavement feels deliberate, with the echoes of footsteps creating a rhythmic pattern. Observing around, one might notice an elderly couple practicing Tai Chi in the park, their movements slow yet deliberate, in harmony with nature. On the other side of the street, a young woman jogs, her breath synchronized with her steps.

Now, why does this setting matter? Why reflect on such ordinary moments? It's in these moments that the essence of life, its simplicity and beauty, is truly felt. An early morning walk isn't just about physical movement; it's a journey of the soul, a meditation, a dance with nature.

By observing these scenes, we are not just bystanders but participants in the grand theatre of life. The elderly couple, the young woman and even the singing birds all share a story, a testament to the wonders of life. This indirect experience, the act of observing without a defined purpose, holds profound wisdom.

It's imperative to understand that some truths aren't directly stated but felt. An early morning walk is an invitation, not just to witness the world waking up but to be a part of this magical transition. As day breaks, it's not the sun that rises, but our consciousness, expanding and embracing the world in all its splendour.

Essay 2:
An Early Morning Walk
(Western Student)

An early morning walk provides unparalleled benefits for both the body and the mind. As one steps out into the fresh morning air, the immediate benefits are evident. The serene environment enhances mental clarity, the brisk walk increases heart rate and metabolism, and the experience serves as a meditation to prepare for the challenges of the day.

First, the lack of distractions in the early hours means a clearer, more focused mindset. The stillness allows for introspection and sets a positive tone for the rest of the day. Research has shown that morning walkers are more likely to be proactive, tackling problems head-on.

Next, the physical benefits are undeniable. Walking increases cardiovascular health, and doing so in the morning can boost metabolism for the day, aiding in weight management. Additionally, exposure to early morning sunlight helps regulate the body's internal biological clock and improves mood.

Furthermore, amidst the hustle and bustle of modern life, an early morning walk offers a moment of meditation. The rhythmic pattern of footsteps, the chirping of birds and the quietude are therapeutic. It's a time to reflect, plan, and simply be.

In conclusion, an early morning walk isn't just an activity; it's an investment in oneself. It ensures mental clarity, physical health and emotional balance. In a world teeming with complexities, it's these simple rituals that offer solace and rejuvenation.

As we can observe, the Western student's essay seeks maximum objectivity, letting facts speak for themselves. The topic is stated at the start and then examples and illustrations proceed to demonstrate the central idea. Chinese texts, however, provide multiple perspectives without stating the topic directly upfront. Understanding these modes of thinking and their influence on translation and writing brings a fresh perspective to the contrast study of Chinese and English and holds immense value in cross-cultural communication.

Do such thinking patterns affect business communication as well? Absolutely. Chen (2015) looked at professional emails and captured the following complaint in Chinese:

> 十月五日第ot-5号合同项下的20万吨大米，原定于十二月底前交货。你放在合同中保证提前交货，并且以此作为签订合同的条件，但是，这批大米迄今尚未装运，对此我们深表遗憾。

Translation into English:

> The 200,000 tons of rice under Contract No. OT-t of 5 October is scheduled to be delivered by the end of December. You have guaranteed an early delivery in the contract, and it is on this understanding that we signed the contract. Up to now, however, the shipment has not yet been made. We very much regret that.

To a native English speaker, this complaint may seem lightweight. The choice for expressing disappointment is 'regret.' A native English speaker is more likely to write something like:

> We are very disappointed to learn that our order for 200,000 tons of rice has not yet been despatched. You guaranteed a delivery date of end-December in our contract,

and we would not have entered into the agreement had we known it would be delayed. Please would you make this delivery by next Monday and confirm this by return email.

This example illustrates how we are trained to seek important information in different parts of texts, such as emails. In the Mandarin version, a native speaker quickly scans the opening sentence about the contract's background, then focuses on the specific details of the delivery situation, noting the final sentence for its implications. If this structure is directly translated into English, a native English speaker might find it confusing. They expect the opening line to clarify the email's purpose, often starting with phrases like "I am writing to ..." In contrast, in Chinese, the background information is crucial to determine responsibility. The reason for writing the email is assumed to be clear, and a solution is expected to be offered implicitly, without an explicit request.

Conversely, if a native English speaker's email, structured according to English norms, is translated into Mandarin, a native Mandarin speaker might perceive it as overly direct and, therefore, somewhat impolite. Thus, successful communication transcends mere language, in terms of vocabulary and grammar. It also involves understanding the customary ways of structuring information in professional writing within that language culture.

SUMMARY

Through this chapter, we see how our very essence is moulded by what we communicate. This symbiosis between thought and language is mirrored in our cerebral processes, reinforcing that language serves not merely as a tool for communication but as the framework shaping our cognition.

While Westerners are analytical, often dissecting problems to their core, Easterners embrace a holistic perspective, seeing the world in its interconnected entirety. Such distinctions, rooted in ancient cultural traditions and societal structures, manifest vividly in studies demonstrating differential grouping patterns among Eastern and Western participants. Such differences are directly reflected in written communication. Chinese writing, influenced by its collective culture, showcases patterns that emphasize the whole over its individual parts, contrasting sharply with the English approach. This difference becomes apparent in everything from word order to sentence structures, revealing the profound impact of culture on communication.

Embracing these revelations is not just an intellectual pursuit; it's a pathway to enhanced understanding, fostering richer global connections and deeper cultural appreciation. Through these insights, we recognize that in the realm of thought and communication, we are truly global citizens, with brains sculpted by the symphony of languages they encounter.

CHAPTER 4

Chinese Communication Styles

Let's turn to the heart of Chinese communication styles and explore how complex relationships between language, culture and interpersonal relationships shape how Chinese people interact with each other.

Chinese communication style is influenced by the cultural norms and values of China. Not surprisingly, there are different approaches by scholars when defining the characteristics of Chinese communication styles. In the following pages, you will be introduced to Western viewpoints and indigenous Chinese interpretations. By offering insights from both Western and Chinese perspectives, we can build a more comprehensive and holistic understanding of Chinese communication styles.

This chapter will equip you with an understanding of the multifaceted nature of Chinese communication styles, from the high-context, indirect and relationship-focused approaches prevalent in Chinese society, to the rich lexical tapestry of the Chinese language itself. You will be better prepared to navigate the complex landscape of Chinese cultural dynamics, fostering deeper connections and more meaningful interactions in the process.

WESTERN PERSPECTIVE — HIGH-CONTEXT COMMUNICATION

We've already established that Chinese communication is often considered 'high-context,' a term coined by anthropologist Edward T. Hall in his seminal work, *Beyond Culture* (1976). In high-context cultures, much of the message is conveyed through nonverbal cues, social norms and shared understanding, rather than explicit words.

Let's take a closer look at the characteristics of China as a high-context communication culture and illustrate how these features manifest in everyday communication and their implications on intercultural understanding. Chinese communication has several key characteristics, including:

- **Reliance on nonverbal cues:** In high-context cultures such as Chinese culture, nonverbal communication, such as facial expressions, body language and gestures, carries significant weight in conveying meaning during conversations. These cues provide additional layers of meaning that complement the spoken language and facilitate understanding.

  In Chinese culture, maintaining eye contact is generally considered a sign of respect and attentiveness. However, the intensity and duration of eye contact may vary depending on the situation and the relationship between the individuals involved. For example, in a business meeting between a manager and a subordinate, the subordinate might avoid maintaining prolonged eye contact with the manager to demonstrate respect and deference.

  During the meeting, the manager may express dissatisfaction with the progress of a project without directly stating it. Instead of explicitly criticizing the subordinate, the manager might raise their eyebrows, purse their lips or subtly shake their head while discussing the project. These nonverbal cues would signal to the subordinate that the manager is not pleased with the progress and expects improvements, without the need for direct confrontation or open criticism.

  The subordinate, understanding the nonverbal cues, would then respond with appropriate facial expressions, such as a slight bow of the head or a concerned look, to acknowledge the manager's concerns and demonstrate their commitment to addressing the issue. In this way, both parties can communicate their thoughts and intentions through nonverbal cues, maintaining harmony and face-saving within the professional relationship.

Imagine a scenario where a foreign business executive is presenting a proposal to a team of Chinese executives. The foreign executive carefully explains the benefits of the proposal, emphasizing the potential profits and long-term growth opportunities. While listening to the presentation, the Chinese executives maintain a neutral facial expression and do not interrupt.

At the end of the presentation, the foreign executive asks for feedback. The most senior Chinese executive gives a slight nod and says, "Your proposal is interesting, and we will consider it carefully." The foreign executive may interpret this response as a positive sign, given the lack of overt disagreement or criticism.

However, in Chinese high-context communication, the nonverbal cues can provide deeper insights into the real opinion of the Chinese executives. During the presentation, the Chinese executives maintained neutral facial expressions, but their body language may have indicated a lack of enthusiasm, such as minimal eye contact, crossed arms or fidgeting.

Moreover, the senior Chinese executive's slight nod could signal a polite way of conveying disapproval without directly stating it. The phrase "we will consider it carefully" may also be an indirect way of saying that they are not convinced by the proposal and are unlikely to move forward with it.

In this example, understanding the nonverbal cues and the indirect communication style is crucial for accurately interpreting the situation and the feedback received. Ignoring or misinterpreting these nonverbal cues could lead to misunderstandings and incorrect assumptions about the Chinese executives' stance on the proposal.

- **Indirectness:** Chinese speakers often use hints, suggestions or metaphorical language to express their thoughts and feelings, rather than stating them outright. This indirectness allows for face-saving and the maintenance of harmony in social interactions.

In Chinese history, there is a famous story about Zhuangzi, the great philosopher who used metaphor to tactfully decline an offer from the emperor. Being too direct could have been perceived as disrespectful, a risky stance with potentially severe consequences. Let's see how he managed this without explicitly saying "no."

One day, the monarch of the state of Chu sent two senior officials to invite Zhuangzi to become an official. Zhuangzi, fishing by the river, asked the officials, "Is there a tortoise enshrined in your state of Chu? It has been dead for three thousand years, its bones placed in a bamboo box, covered with beautiful cloth. May I ask, does the tortoise prefer being honoured posthumously, or would it have liked to be alive, wading in the mud with its tail wagging?" The officials immediately replied that it would prefer rolling in the mud. Zhuangzi then said, "Yes, I too wish to live and roll in the mud."

Zhuangzi compared his desire for freedom to the tortoise's in a way that the officials could understand and even sympathize with. He subtly conveyed that one loses their free will when serving the emperor. Without outright rejecting the offer, the officials fully accepted his reasoning. This story illustrates how sometimes you can communicate your refusal through tactful hints, allowing the other party to understand your intentions without directly blaming you.

- **Emphasis on relationships:** High-context cultures place great importance on developing and maintaining interpersonal relationships. Building and maintaining relationships, or *guanxi*, is crucial in Chinese culture. Communication styles often focus on fostering personal connections and trust, with an emphasis on mutual reciprocity and loyalty. Chinese culture places great importance on respecting authority and social hierarchy. Communication styles often reflect this by demonstrating deference, politeness and formality when interacting with people of higher status or older age.

  Chinese individuals are also taught to be modest and to prioritize moral integrity and credibility in their interactions. This approach isn't just for personal virtue – it often leads to success in both careers and social settings. As Chen (1997) notes, a lasting relationship can pave the way for countless future business opportunities. Contrary to Western views where a deal often signals the end of an association, in China, it's just the beginning of a lasting personal connection.

  It's essential to understand that the act of doing business in China isn't just a transaction. Going into an arrangement purely for profit is seen as cold and potentially damaging to interpersonal relations (Huang et al., 1994). What's prized in Chinese culture is a business that strengthens the bond between individuals. And these bonds? They're resilient. Even if a particular venture fails, the personal relationship remains, leaving the door open for future collaborations. Conversely, a successful deal without a strong relationship foundation doesn't guarantee future collaborations.

- **Importance of context:** High-context cultures rely on contextual factors, such as the speaker's identity, the listener's relationship to the speaker and the social situation, to help interpret the meaning behind words and actions.

  Our relationship is a key contextual factor in understanding each other's intended meaning. Imagine sending a message to your friend of many years, Wang, inviting him to a party at your home. Wang replies, "I'll try my best to come." In the context of your close friendship, you understand that Wang's response means he genuinely intends to attend the event and will make an effort to do so. The phrase "I'll try my best" reflects Wang's casual tone and the understanding between two friends.

  Now, consider a different scenario where you are the head of a department and invite one of your senior colleagues, Zhang, to an important work event. Zhang responds with the same phrase, "I'll try my best to come." In this professional context, with the hierarchical relationship between you and Zhang, the meaning of Zhang's response might be different. Instead of expressing genuine intention, Zhang's reply could be an indirect way of saying that he is not certain about attending the event, possibly due to other commitments or priorities. In this case, the phrase "I'll try my best" acts as a polite and indirect way of expressing uncertainty without directly declining the invitation.

  In both examples, the same phrase is used, but the meaning changes based on the contextual factors, such as the relationship between the speakers and the social situation. Understanding the context is crucial for accurately interpreting messages in Chinese communication, as it allows the listener to grasp the true meaning behind the words and adapt their response accordingly.

The Chinese complaint letter in Chapter 3 was notably indirect, not explicitly asking for a resolution. Instead, it went to great lengths describing the context of the situation, such as the broken delivery promise. Why is this? In Chinese culture, context is paramount. In the Chinese mindset, the circumstances of what has occurred often speak louder than words.

- **Preservation of harmony:** High-context communication cultures prioritize maintaining social harmony and avoiding confrontation or conflict. We have discussed the importance of interpersonal relationships but be aware that this is not just on an individual level. Chinese communication styles prioritize group harmony and the needs of the community over individual interests. This can result in communication patterns that emphasize consensus-building, cooperation and avoiding direct confrontation.

Understanding China's high-context communication culture has important implications for intercultural communication and relationship-building. By appreciating the nuances of Chinese communication styles, individuals from low-context cultures can better adapt their communication strategies to effectively navigate social and professional interactions with Chinese counterparts. This adaptation can lead to more productive and harmonious relationships, facilitating intercultural understanding and collaboration. We will explore this further in later chapters.

CHINESE PERSPECTIVE – LEXICAL APPROACH

Having explained high-context communication of Chinese culture from a Western perspective, let's now turn to Chinese scholars and how they define the characteristics of Chinese-style communication. Gao and Ting-Toomey (1998) in their book *Communicating Effectively with the Chinese*, used a lexical approach explaining the characteristics of Chinese communication styles. It is worthwhile mentioning this approach, as it explains the Chinese communication style via Chinese language. Below is the summary of the key concepts being mentioned in their book:

1. 含蓄 (hánxù, indirectness)
2. 听话 (tīnghuà, listening-centeredness)
3. 客气 (kèqì , politeness)
4. 自己人 (zìjǐ rén, the insider effect)

The first concept is 含蓄 (hánxù, translated as indirectness, a concept we've discussed. In Chinese, 含 means to withhold, and 蓄 means to store. This is very telling, right? You do not express explicitly. Instead, you leave space for interpretation. As mentioned previously, Chinese people believe that communication is, and should be, indirect. This allows both the speaker and hearer to save face if necessary. A successful communicator is someone who can say something with just the right level of directness so that the listener understands. And a smart communicator is also the person (if a listener) to get the intended meaning without the speaker being explicit. In Chinese, this level of communication is considered a form of art. Nothing is being said, but everything is understood. This is not easy, even for Chinese themselves. Therefore, this leads to the second concept: 听话 (tīnghuà, listening-centeredness).

One could argue that 听话 (listening-centeredness) is a characteristic of Chinese communication style, or rather, it is a must-have strategy. 听话 literally means 'listen to the words,' but it actually goes far beyond that. In their book, Gao and Ting-Toomey argue for another important dimension of 听话 (listening-centeredness). They argue that as Chinese society is hierarchical, there are conditions associated with speaking and not everyone is entitled to speak. They quote examples of a boss with a subordinate, and parents with children to demonstrate how an asymmetrical style of communication exists in Chinese culture due to the influence of Confucian values. The more power, or more experience one has, the more right they have to speak. The others would then need to learn to 听 – to listen to what's been said. It does not just mean to listen attentively but also to do what's been asked of them.

An indirect communication style, coupled with a tendency to defer to superiors, often makes it difficult for Chinese individuals to openly express their true thoughs and feelings. For instance, in Chinese schools, pupils are taught to 听话, which translates to 'do as you are told,' rather than to question or challenge authority. Consequently, in UK higher education, universities often find it more challenging to encourage Chinese students to participate and speak up in class, compared to their EU counterparts. While there is a shift occurring, the traditional approach to education in China emphasises listening to the teacher and absorbing their teachings, as opposed to questioning, debating or challenging the teacher's views. This dynamic is also prevalent in the workplace.

Politeness (客气, kèqì) is the third characteristic mentioned by Gao and Ting-Toomey. The word 客气 (kèqì) breaks down in Chinese to mean 'guest' and 'atmosphere.' This is telling, as it informs us it is the type of politeness that is expected in guest-host situations. As a host, you are expected to welcome your guests at the entrance of your office building and see them off by walking them to the exit; you are expected to prepare food and drinks generously; you are also expected to play down the effort you put into the preparation to ensure the guests don't feel embarrassed or indebted to you. As a guest, you are expected to reject the invitation initially to avoid causing trouble to the host. After you've done this at least two or three times (to be certain the invite is genuine), you will then be expected to bring gifts. Show your appreciation by complimenting the food and demonstrate the generosity of the host by not finishing everything on your plate. You must also invite the host to be your guest next time.

Of course, politeness goes beyond the guest-host situation. Gao and Ting-Toomy considered being modest part of 客气 (politeness). They provided some examples of language refinement for the purpose of demonstrating humility. I would argue the translation of 客气 as politeness is not wrong, but it is not complete.

The final characteristic mentioned by Gao and Ting-Toomy is 自己人 (zìjǐ rén), which they call the 'insider effect' of communication. This is an interesting and important perspective. Gao and Ting-Toomy introduced this concept when asking why Americans have such different experiences with Chinese people when visiting China. American visitors found strangers on the street rude and careless but found their Chinese friends warm and polite. Gao and Ting-Toomy attribute the reason for such contradictory behaviour to the 'insider effect.' They argue that in Chinese culture, as a collectivism culture, the notion of in-group (insider) relationships is far more important than out-group (outsider) ones. This is because insider groups often serve as the primary, ongoing units of sociation and network of each person. Therefore, Chinese people make a clear distinction between insiders and outsiders.

As a result, their communication behaviour also adapts and changes. For example, you are not expected to say "thank you" or "please" to your family. This is a real-life struggle for me. I am lucky to have an Italian partner who cooks well. Now that we've been together for many years, my Chinese insider effect has kicked in and I no longer say, "thank you" or "please" when he has cooked dinner for me. He complains from time to time, saying, "You know you are not in a restaurant." I answer back, "Exactly – it's *because* I am not in a restaurant."

This phenomenon is not unique to Chinese culture. It is evident in other languages and cultures as well. Eisenstein and Bodman (1993) examined linguistic behaviour of expressing gratitude in the US, and recorded a similar incident. A Puerto Rican woman, who had been living in the US for many years, was visited by her father. During the stay, he helped take care of her son (his grandson). When she thanked him, he became angry and felt hurt. Her mother asked: "How could you have been so thoughtless? You thanked your father. He was happy to take care of Jonnie. Have you forgotten how to behave? He's your father and he loves you. How could you be so cold – to thank him?"

Even saying "thank you" can be offensive. A lot of this is to do with what we perceive our roles to be in relation to the people we interact with. In Chinese culture, if you act more politely than expected, you may be told "不要见外" (Bùyào jiàn wài), "你太见外了" (nǐ tài jiàn wài le), meaning "don't be an outsider" or "you are too polite."

The insider effect impacts Chinese communication in several ways:

- **Language and expressions:** Insiders often use more informal, colloquial language and share in-jokes or local expressions that may not be understood by outsiders. In contrast, communication with outsiders is generally more formal and adheres to standard language conventions.

- **Directness and indirectness:** With insiders, Chinese individuals may be more direct and open in expressing their thoughts and feelings, as the close relationship allows for a greater degree of trust and understanding. However, when communicating with outsiders, Chinese people tend to be more indirect, using hints, euphemisms or nonverbal cues to convey their intentions. This indirect communication style helps maintain harmony, save face and avoid potential conflict.

- **Nonverbal communication:** Insiders may rely more on nonverbal cues and shared understanding to communicate, as they can often accurately interpret each other's gestures, facial expressions and body language. On the other hand, with outsiders, nonverbal cues may be less emphasized, with more importance placed on spoken words and formal etiquette.

- **Information sharing:** In Chinese culture, trust is a crucial factor in determining the level of information sharing. Insiders often share more personal information, opinions and experiences with each other, while communication with outsiders may be more reserved and focused on general or neutral topics.

Understanding the insider effect on communication in Chinese culture is essential for successfully navigating social and professional interactions. By recognizing the distinctions between insiders and outsiders and adjusting communication styles accordingly, individuals can foster more effective intercultural communication and build stronger relationships within Chinese culture. Building any new relationship, you will find the moment when both parties perhaps feel comfortable using '你' (nǐ) instead of '您' (nín). Do not be offended if your Chinese colleagues stop using "thank you" or "please." It may not be a reflection of them forgetting their manners, it might just be a sign that they feel close with you.

NONVERBAL COMMUNICATION

As stated, nonverbal communication plays a vital part in Chinese communication. It often provides context, reinforces verbal messages, and conveys emotions and interpersonal attitudes. It can manifest in many forms like body language, facial expressions, gestures and even silence. Let's explore some specific aspects of nonverbal communication in Chinese culture.

- **Facial Expressions:** Chinese culture values the ability to control and mask emotions and, as such, facial expressions might not be as overt as in other cultures. Smiling is a common nonverbal cue, but it might not always denote happiness; it can also be a way to mask discomfort or embarrassment.

  Example: If someone gives an inappropriate gift, the recipient may still smile to avoid making the gift-giver uncomfortable, even though they might feel awkward or embarrassed.

- **Eye Contact:** In general, eye contact is considered necessary and polite. However, direct eye contact is less common in Chinese culture, especially among the older generation or in formal settings. It is often seen as a sign of disrespect or a challenge to authority if a subordinate holds direct eye contact with a supervisor.

Example: A student might avoid making direct eye contact with a teacher during a scolding to show respect and acknowledgement of their mistake.

- **Gestures and Body Language:** Some common Chinese gestures differ significantly from those in Western cultures. For instance, beckoning someone is done with the palm facing down, waving the fingers toward oneself. Also, pointing with an index finger is often considered impolite, so people might use an open hand instead.

- **Touch:** Physical touch between people who aren't close friends or family is often minimal in Chinese culture. Public displays of affection are less common and can sometimes be frowned upon.

- **Personal Space and Proximity:** Chinese culture often involves a closer personal space in conversation than some Western cultures. However, this is dependent on the closeness of the relationship.

- **Silence:** Maintaining silence holds a significant role in Chinese communication. It can serve as an acknowledgement, a sign of respect or a method to avoid conflict.

Understanding these nonverbal cues can greatly aid effective communication and help avoid misunderstandings when interacting with individuals from Chinese culture.

SUMMARY

Diving into the labyrinth of high-context communication, this chapter explores the intricate patterns of Chinese communication. In China, a high-context society, verbal communication is just the tip of the iceberg. Beneath the surface lies many nonverbal cues, shared understandings and implicit messages, all working harmoniously to convey the true essence of a message. Whether it's a slight nod from a senior executive or the gentle phrase, "We will consider it carefully," the Chinese prefer to communicate with subtlety and grace, prioritizing interpersonal bonds and societal harmony.

In professional settings, indirect communication in China is a strategic tool, used to build credibility and promote societal harmony. The relationship-centric nature of Chinese business interactions challenges the Western notion that a deal marks the end of a relationship; in China, it's merely the beginning.

Drilling down further, the lexical approach, as explained by Gao and Ting-Toomey, sheds light on key concepts underpinning Chinese communication, like 'politeness' and 'the insider effect.' The latter beautifully elucidates the nuanced differences in how the Chinese communicate with insiders versus outsiders. From the choice of language to the degree of information shared, these distinctions play a crucial role in shaping intercultural interactions.

By understanding these subtle nuances, you are now better poised to navigate intercultural journeys, forging deeper connections and fostering mutual respect.

CHAPTER 5

Digital Communication in China

Digital communication is a fundamental part of today's global business. So, how does digital communication function in China? How does it compare to the West? Which social media apps should you be familiar with when doing business in China? And what cultural considerations do you need to adopt when involving digital communication? These are the topics we will explore in this chapter.

E-COMMUNICATION INSTRUMENTS IN INTERCULTURAL BUSINESS COMMUNICATION IN CHINA

In today's global business world, face-to-face chats are often swapped out for online messages and meetings. There are many ways to connect, such as email, WhatsApp, Skype, Google Meet, WebEx and more. However, in China, things can be quite different. Owing to stringent internet censorship for political reasons—a subject often debated—the Great Firewall of China, pivotal to this censorship system, complicates online communication with other countries. Consequently, some widely used, legal and nonpolitical internet services like Google are not accessible in China.

As a result, popular communication tools such as WhatsApp and Google Meet can be challenging to use. Chinese users frequently resort to VPNs, technology that circumvents the Great Firewall, to access otherwise restricted tools. However, VPNs are not free, and internet connectivity can be unreliable. Therefore, when conducting business with Chinese companies, the Great Firewall is a crucial factor to consider in selecting appropriate internet tools for communication. So, what types of communication methods are predominantly used by Chinese businesspeople? What are the most effective tools for Chinese businesspeople in intercultural business communication?

This was precisely what researchers at Universiti Teknologi Malaysia looked into in 2021. They conducted interviews at an international software company in Beijing, aiming to discover the reasons behind Chinese employees' preferences for intercultural business communication tools. Research revealed that the communication preferences of Chinese business employees demonstrate a nuanced approach to selecting the right tools based on the context and urgency of their message. Here are the key insights:

- **Preference for Email and Instant Messaging:** Emails and instant messages, primarily through WeChat, WhatsApp and Skype, are the primary modes of daily communication. The choice between these depends on the formality and urgency of the matter.

- **Email for Formality and Nonurgent Matters:** Emails are preferred for formal announcements and situations where immediate responses are not critical. This tool is also favoured for sending files.

- **Combining Email with Instant Messages:** To address the challenge of counterparts not checking emails regularly, Chinese businesspersons often follow up with instant messages to alert them about important emails.

- **Instant Messages for Direct, One-to-One Communication:** For quick, direct communication, instant messaging is preferred, especially for one-to-one interactions.

- **Voice Communication in Specific Scenarios:** Voice communication is less favoured due to difficulties in understanding accents and self-confidence in speaking English. It is, however, used in emergencies for quick confirmations, or to explain complex issues that are too cumbersome to type out.

- **Voice Communication in Informal Settings:** Informal training and discussions may occur through voice communication via instant messaging services, especially when text explanations are inadequate.

- **Using Video Conferencing for Group and Formal Situations:** For formal occasions or situations involving multiple participants, platforms like Google Meet, Tencent Meeting and Zoom are employed for meetings and presentations.

As Chinese employees prefer to receive replies quickly to complete tasks in the shortest possible time, they send emails to counterparts and expect immediate responses. If they do not receive a timely reply, instant messaging tools like WeChat, WhatsApp or Skype are used as reminders. Regarding relationship outcomes, although Chinese employees consider face-to-face communication the best way to establish relationships with others, instant messaging tools are also preferred for building relationships because they allow for quick responses and maintain a casual conversation atmosphere. The use of emojis is found to be helpful in creating a friendly and relaxed chat environment, facilitating easier relationship development.

When addressing cultural adjustment, cultural differences are most pronounced in instant messaging and emails. Cultural conflicts commonly occur in these mediums. However, instant messaging tools are seen as the fastest way to adapt to a new cultural fit between interactants. Furthermore, most cultural differences and misunderstandings arise when communicating through emails. Instant messaging allows for immediate resolution of misunderstandings, while emails often require more extensive explanation.

The above research findings show us a strategic approach to communication by Chinese businesspeople, balancing efficiency, clarity and respect for formal protocols, tailored to the unique challenges and preferences of Chinese business environments.

SOCIAL MEDIA'S RESHAPING OF CHINESE BUSINESS COMMUNICATION

In an era where digital interconnectivity reigns supreme, the impact of social media on global business communication is undeniable. But in China, a country with its own digital eco-system and sociocultural nuances, the transformation driven by social media in the realm of business communication has been both profound and distinctive. In the coming pages, let's explore the dynamics of how social media platforms have redefined Chinese business communication.

ACCELERATED SPEED OF COMMUNICATION

Platforms like WeChat and Weibo have made real-time com-munication the norm in China. Businesses can relay infor-mation, receive feedback and respond to inquiries instantly. This immediacy has made Chinese businesses more agile and responsive, allowing them to adapt to market changes at an unprecedented pace.

For example, Luckin Coffee, a Chinese coffeehouse chain, frequently uses WeChat to send immediate promotions and flash deals, leveraging the platform's wide reach and real-time engagement capabilities.

PERSONALIZATION AND DIRECT ENGAGEMENT

In the past, Chinese businesses relied heavily on formal B2B or B2C channels for communication. Now, social media has blurred these lines, allowing businesses to engage directly and personally with their customers. Brands often employ influencers or 'Key Opinion Leaders' (KOLs) to endorse products, creating a more personal, relatable touch to their marketing strategies.

OPPO, a smartphone brand, frequently collaborates with celebrities and KOLs in China to create personalized campaigns on platforms like Weibo, thus connecting directly with younger audiences. Perfect Diary, one of China's most popular cosmetic brands, effectively uses KOLs to promote their products. Collaborating with local influencers allows the brand to present their products in a more personalized and relatable manner.

Case Study:
Michael Kors' Success with
Key Opinion Leader Yang Mi in China

Introduction: Michael Kors, an American luxury fashion company, recognized the significant potential of the Chinese market and the value of local influencers or KOLs in shaping consumer opinion.

Background: By the mid-2010s, China's luxury market was booming, driven by a rising middle class with increasing disposable income. However, competition was intense, with several international luxury brands vying for attention. To differentiate itself and make a mark, Michael Kors turned to the power of KOLs.

Strategy: Partner with renowned Chinese actress and singer, Yang Mi, who has a massive following in China, especially among younger consumers.

Implementation:
1. **Brand Ambassador:** In 2017, Yang Mi was announced as the first global brand ambassador for Michael Kors.
2. **Exclusive Collection:** Michael Kors launched the 'Whitney' handbag, codesigned with Yang Mi. This collaboration was marketed as the 'Yang Mi x Michael Kors' collection.
3. **Social Media Engagement:** Yang Mi frequently showcased her Michael Kors outfits and accessories on her Weibo account, which boasted millions of followers.
4. **Special Events:** Yang Mi made appearances at Michael Kors shows during global fashion weeks, further amplifying the brand's visibility among her fans.

Outcome:
1. **Increased Brand Visibility:** Michael Kors saw a surge in its brand mentions and online searches in China after the partnership.
2. **Sales Boost:** The 'Whitney' handbag quickly became a best-seller in China, with several outlets reporting stock shortages.
3. **Engagement:** Michael Kors' social media platforms, especially Weibo and WeChat, saw increased engagement rates, with many posts related to Yang Mi garnering significantly higher likes and shares.
4. **Recognition:** The collaboration was recognized as one of the successful Western Business – KOL partnerships in China, serving as a case study for other brands looking to make inroads into the Chinese luxury market.

Conclusion: Michael Kors' partnership with Yang Mi underscores the immense influence of KOLs in the Chinese market. The collaboration not only bolstered the brand's visibility but also drove tangible sales results, demonstrating the potent combination of brand and influencer in resonating with the Chinese audience.

ENHANCED TRANSPARENCY

Customer reviews, comments and live streams have given consumers a voice like never before. While this increases accountability for businesses, it also offers them an opportunity to showcase transparency, address concerns head-on and build trust in real-time.

After a scandal related to substandard products, Daigou traders – individuals who purchase goods overseas to resell in China – began using social media to showcase the authenticity and quality of their products, filming their shopping sprees to build trust.

A SHIFT TO VISUAL AND MULTIMEDIA CONTENT

Platforms such as Douyin (the Chinese version of TikTok) have emphasized the importance of visual storytelling. Businesses now leverage short videos, interactive polls and augmented reality features to engage with their audience, making communication more dynamic and engaging. ByteDance, the company behind Douyin (TikTok outside of China), regularly collaborates with businesses to create visually engaging advertising campaigns that leverage the platform's unique format.

LOCALIZATION OF GLOBAL BRANDS

For international brands seeking a foothold in the Chinese market, social media has been instrumental in understanding local preferences and cultural nuances. By engaging with local influencers and tailoring content for Chinese social media platforms, global brands can resonate more deeply with Chinese consumers. KFC in China, rather than relying solely on its global image, embraced local Chinese cultural elements on social media, such as Lunar New Year promotions and Mid-Autumn Festival special menus. Starbucks collaborated with Tencent to introduce a social gifting feature on WeChat, allowing users to send Starbucks gifts to friends, tapping into the Chinese cultural norm of gift-giving.

EVOLUTION OF E-COMMERCE

Platforms like Taobao and JD.com have integrated social features, transforming shopping from a solitary activity into a social experience. Shoppers can now view live demonstrations, interact with sellers in real-time and share products with their social circles, all within the platform. Luxury brand Burberry launched its Lunar New Year campaign through a Tmall (a Chinese retail website) livestream, giving fans a closer, behind-the-scenes look at their products and generating immediate online sales. On platforms like Taobao, stores often employ livestream hosts who showcase products in real-time. Cosmetic brand MAC sold over 10,000 lipsticks in five minutes through a livestreaming session on Taobao, highlighting the effectiveness of this form of e-commerce.

WHEN THINGS GO WRONG

Social media's viral nature means that any business mishap can quickly escalate. Chinese businesses have had to become adept at online reputation management, addressing issues and crises proactively to maintain brand integrity. Dolce and Gabbana faced a social media storm in China after airing an advertisement that many Chinese netizens deemed racist. Their mishandling of the subsequent backlash, including derogatory comments, escalated the crisis. The situation emphasized the importance of adept crisis management in the age of social media.

Case Study:
Dolce and Gabbana's Crisis in China
– A Social Media Misstep

Introduction: The digital age offers vast opportunities for brands to connect with audiences worldwide. Yet, with great power comes great responsibility. A brand's reputation can be jeopardized with just a single misguided action. Dolce and Gabbana's recent crisis in China serves as a stark reminder.

The Event: Dolce and Gabbana, an esteemed fashion house, had planned an extravagant fashion show in Shanghai on 22 November, 2018, titled the "Great Fashion Show." A stellar lineup of 350 models, over 40 celebrities, and 1,500 invited guests were set to grace the event. However, what should have been a celebration of fashion turned into an overnight PR nightmare.

The Trigger: A series of promotional videos, "Eating with Chopsticks," was launched on Chinese microblog Weibo and Instagram on 17 November. The videos depicted an Asian woman attempting to eat Italian dishes such as pizza and spaghetti with chopsticks. Chinese viewers instantly deemed this as a demeaning portrayal, perpetuating stereotypes and racial undertones.

The controversy intensified when alleged derogatory comments about China from label cofounder Stefano Gabbana surfaced on Instagram. Though Gabbana and the brand cited a hacked account for these comments, the damage was done.

The Fallout: Prominent Chinese celebrities and KOLs swiftly distanced themselves from the brand. Personalities such as Zhang Ziyi, Li Bingbing and Huang Xiaoming expressed their displeasure, boycotting the upcoming show and the brand altogether. Key Chinese e-commerce stores, like Alibaba and Jindong, delisted Dolce and Gabbana products, dealing a further blow to the brand's image and bottom line.

By 23 November, founders Domenico Dolce and Stefano Gabbana issued a personal video apology, uttering the phrase, "Dui Bu Qi!" ["We apologize!"]

Reflection: How could a global brand, with a significant presence in China, miscalculate the implications of such content? With 56 stores across 12 Chinese cities since its 2006 entry, the company should have recognized the importance of cultural sensitivity.

A Bain and Co. report highlighted that Chinese customers contributed to almost one-third of global luxury goods spending in 2017. The Chinese market's potential is colossal. Yet, like the Chinese proverb suggests, "Water can hold the boat up, but it can also flip it over." [水能载舟，亦能覆舟, Shuǐ néng zài zhōu, yì néng fù zhōu.]

Conclusion: Brands must tread carefully, especially when navigating diverse cultural waters. Dolce and Gabbana's experience underscores the need for brands to cultivate genuine respect and understanding for the cultures they serve. It's not just about marketing; it's about forging real connections and demonstrating genuine respect. In a world where one misstep can echo around the globe, cultural sensitivity isn't optional – it's essential.

DATA-DRIVEN DECISION-MAKING

The analytics provided by social media platforms furnish businesses with insights into customer preferences, behaviours and sentiments. This data-driven approach allows businesses to tailor their communication strategies more effectively and predict market trends. Alibaba Group harnesses the power of big data analytics across its platforms. With these insights, merchants on Tmall or Taobao can understand buyer preferences and adjust their offerings accordingly, resulting in more targeted and effective marketing campaigns.

These examples highlight the complex relationship between businesses and social media in China. When tapped into effectively, platforms like WeChat, Douyin and Taobao offer not just outreach but profound insights, allowing businesses to evolve and cater to the dynamic Chinese market.

In conclusion, social media has not merely influenced Chinese business communication; it has revolutionized it. While the digital landscape offers unparalleled opportunities, it also comes with its challenges. For businesses to thrive in this new era, they must be adaptable, authentic and ever-aware of the evolving digital zeitgeist. With its unique blend of culture, technology and commerce, China stands as a testament to the transformative power of social media in the business world.

WECHAT — THE BEDROCK OF BUSINESS COMMUNICATIONS

Since the internet's advent, numerous platforms have emerged, revolutionizing how we communicate, socialize and conduct business. In China, this revolution has a standout example: WeChat. The latest statistics show that in 2023, there are 827.2 million WeChat users in China, which accounts for 58.9% of the total population.

For many Chinese, living without WeChat is unimaginable, and that is no exaggeration. I wouldn't know how to communicate with my parents or collaborate with Chinese partners without WeChat. In this section, we will look at the multifaceted nature of WeChat and examine its indispensable role in business communication in China.

Understanding WeChat

At its core, WeChat (known as "Weixin" in China) is a messaging app. However, labelling it just as a messaging app doesn't do justice to its extensive capabilities. Launched in 2011 by Tencent, one of China's largest tech companies, WeChat started as a mobile messaging platform but quickly morphed into an all-encompassing super-app.

Apart from standard messaging, it offers features like voice and video calls, social media functions through 'Moments,' a built-in wallet, mini-programs (which are akin to apps within the app), and various services ranging from ride-hailing to food delivery. With over a billion monthly active users, it's not just a communication tool; it's an integral part of the daily lives of Chinese citizens.

WECHAT'S ROLE IN BUSINESS COMMUNICATION

- **Unified Communication Channel:** WeChat has replaced emails and traditional calls as the primary mode of business communication in China. From quick chats to formal discussions, from sharing files to conducting video conferences, WeChat provides a unified platform that streamlines various communication needs. Consider a Beijing-based manufacturing company, which can negotiate deals with suppliers from different part of China, gets updates from its factory floor, and communicates with its sales team all through WeChat.

Instead of using emails, which may take longer to get a response, or making phone calls, they use WeChat groups for immediate feedback. This is especially handy during times of urgent decision-making.

- **WeChat Official Accounts:** Companies of all sizes can create official accounts on WeChat. These accounts allow businesses to communicate with their followers, share updates, and even set up e-commerce functionalities. This direct line of communication fosters customer engagement and loyalty. For example, like many other international businesses, Starbucks China has an official account on WeChat. Through this account, they not only share new product launches and promotions, but also allow customers to gift Starbucks products to friends, directly via WeChat. This direct line of communication enhances their customer engagement and loyalty. KFC in China is another great example. Through their WeChat official account, they not only run promotions but also share stories that resonate with Chinese traditions and values. During the Mid-Autumn Festival, instead of merely promoting their products, they shared stories about the importance of family reunions during this festival. Such content made them culturally relevant and deepened their connection with Chinese consumers.

- **WeChat Pay:** One of WeChat's standout features is its built-in digital wallet. Businesses can integrate WeChat Pay, allowing them to conduct transactions seamlessly. From a consumer buying a product to businesses settling invoices, the financial dimension of business communication is facilitated flawlessly. Even beggars on the street ask you to WeChat Pay them. When it was first launched, a boutique hotel in Shanghai allowed tourists to pay for their accommodation and services using WeChat Pay. Tourists, especially those from other parts of China, preferred this method over credit cards or cash. All they need is their mobile phone, which also gives them an instant digital receipt. Nowadays, all hotels in major Chinese cities accept such payment options.

- **Mini-Programs:** These are sub-applications within the WeChat ecosystem. They can be developed for myriad business needs, from e-commerce platforms to interactive customer service bots. For businesses, mini-programs negate the need to create standalone apps, saving resources and ensuring they remain within the WeChat environment, along with their customers. McDonald's China launched a mini-program on WeChat that allows users to order and pay for meals so that customers can pick up their orders without waiting in a queue. This mini-program not only offers customer convenience but also streamlines the restaurant's operations during peak hours.

- **QR Code Integration:** The pervasive use of QR codes in China can largely be attributed to WeChat. Businesses can generate QR codes for various purposes – for people to follow their official accounts, to make payments or to access specific content. This has made interactions and transactions more dynamic and interactive. In historical cities such as Chengdu, many local artisans who make custom jewellery set up a stall at a weekend market. Instead of having a card machine or dealing with cash transactions, they display a QR code for their WeChat accounts. Customers scan the code, make the payment and receive an instant digital confirmation. This not only simplifies the transaction but also enables artisans to stay connected with customers for future promotions or custom orders. This method is also popular with event organizers and educators.

THE CULTURAL SIGNIFICANCE

To truly understand WeChat's dominance in business communications, one has to look at the cultural nuances. As already established, in China, business is not just about transactions; it's about relationships. The term *Guanxi* encapsulates the sophisticated web of relationships and the importance of maintaining them in a business context, which is a concept we will explore in Chapter 8.

WeChat, with its blend of professional and personal communication tools, aligns perfectly with this ethos. It's not uncommon for business partners in China to share moments from their personal lives, exchange holiday greetings and discuss other nonbusiness topics before delving into professional matters. WeChat's versatile platform ensures that this blend of the personal and professional happens seamlessly.

For a Western company, understanding and respecting this blending of personal and professional realms is crucial. Engage in the culture, participate in local festivals or traditions, and use WeChat to showcase this engagement. It's not about token gestures but genuine integration and respect for Chinese traditions and values.

CHALLENGES AND CONSIDERATIONS

While WeChat's role in business communication is undeniable, it's not without challenges. The app's pervasiveness means that the line between work and personal life can blur. Additionally, as with all digital platforms, data security and privacy concerns persist.

Jason, an American businessman, moved to China to expand his tech startup. Initially, he kept most of his interactions formal and via email, as was his practice in the US. However, he soon noticed his Chinese counterparts were sharing holiday photos, festival wishes or even daily life snippets on WeChat. Jason was used to keeping his private and professional lives separate, so he initially found it difficult. However, as he spent more time in China, he managed to adapt and strike a balance. He also became more familiar with the private settings of WeChat, which allow him to adjust his use of WeChat to a more conformable and sustainable level.

It is not always easy to reach a sustainable level. The 996-working culture in China really can push the line between work and personal life to the limit. People can contact you 24/7 via WeChat messages. With the time difference between China and where you are, it can be very difficult. A balanced approach is required to avoid exhausting yourself with the need to respond quickly. You need to set boundaries with cultural sensitivity, so you don't offend others.

Moreover, foreign businesses operating in China need to be aware of the cultural and regulatory landscape surrounding WeChat. This includes understanding censorship rules, data-handling practices, and the nuances of digital etiquette in a Chinese business context.

Sophie, a European entrepreneur, started an e-commerce platform in China. She heavily relied on WeChat for business but found her account temporarily blocked once due to a misunderstanding over content she shared. It was considered as spam instead of normal business activity.

Western companies need to be aware of content guidelines. This goes beyond not discussing sensitive political issues. Regular audits, training sessions for team members and even hiring local experts can ensure smoother operations on WeChat. Also, recognize the dominant features and services within WeChat and see how your company can complement rather than compete against them.

UTILIZING WECHAT FOR A WESTERN COMPANY:

What is the best way to utilize WeChat as a Western Company? Here are some tips:

1. ***Guanxi* Matters:** While business in the West often prioritizes efficiency and directness, in China, building relationships is fundamental. Use WeChat not just for transactions but to cultivate relationships. Try to get your key clients or contact person in China on your WeChat friend list.

2. **Localize Content:** It's not enough to translate content to Chinese; it needs to resonate with local values, traditions and trends. Use WeChat Moments or Official Accounts to share content that showcases your brand's understanding and respect for Chinese culture.

3. **Integration with WeChat Pay:** Given its vast user base, integrating with WeChat Pay can boost sales and offer convenience to customers.

4. **Use Mini-Programs Smartly:** Instead of trying to drive traffic away from WeChat to your app or website, consider developing mini-programs within WeChat for e-commerce, customer service or other functionalities.

5. **Stay Updated with Guidelines:** WeChat, being a Chinese platform, has specific content and operational guidelines. Regularly update yourself to avoid any inadvertent missteps.

6. **Engage with Local Influencers:** Collaborate with KOLs on WeChat to reach a wider audience and gain credibility.

In conclusion, while WeChat offers a vast landscape of opportunities, it's vital to approach it with cultural sensitivity, adaptability and an understanding of its unique ecosystem. By doing so, Western companies can thrive in China's dynamic market. For businesses, understanding and integrating into the WeChat ecosystem isn't just an advantage; it's a necessity. It's not just about keeping up with communication trends but about immersing oneself in the heart of Chinese business culture. If you haven't used it before, it's time to download and start getting connected with your Chinese partners and friends.

SUMMARY

In this chapter, we have explored the transformative effects of social media platforms on business communication in China, a country with unique digital and sociocultural dynamics. I have shown you research on preferred digital communication channels in China. We have also observed the revolutionary impact of social media, particularly WeChat, on Chinese business communication. For businesses to succeed in this new landscape, adaptability, authenticity and sensitivity to the local culture are paramount.

PART TWO

The 'Why'

CHAPTER 6

Chinese Beliefs about Communication

Welcome to Part Two of the book, where we explore the invisible part of the Chinese cultural iceberg and peel away the cultural layers so we can understand the rationale behind Chinese communication.

At the heart of every culture lies a complex web of beliefs, traditions and norms that guide the behaviour of its people. Communication, as an intrinsic facet of human interaction, is no exception to this rule. For many, the essence of communication is shaped by myriad factors ranging from personal experiences to deep-rooted cultural ideologies. In the case of China, a civilization with thousands of years of recorded history, understanding communication demands a voyage back in time.

From the days of Confucian classrooms to modern boardrooms, how have traditional Chinese beliefs moulded the way communication is perceived? How do age-old proverbs still dictate the nuances of a conversation, and how do they align with modern context?

UNDERCOVER CHINESE BELIEFS ON COMMUNICATION VIA IDIOMS AND PROVERBS

Contemporary concepts do not form in isolation, but rather carry insights that are passed down through dynasties. We all harbour beliefs about communication, whether they revolve around the nuances of articulation, the importance of unsaid words or the role of nonverbal cues. Such beliefs not only define our individual perspectives but also shape collective cultural standpoints on the nature and function of communication.

As previously explained, language is a cultural product. So, we will explore Chinese beliefs about communication through the world of Chinese idioms. Idioms, or '成语' (*chéngyǔ*), are not mere linguistic constructs in Chinese culture; they are the vessels that carry the philosophies, stories and morals cultivated over thousands of years. You will see how Chinese idioms reveal the nation's beliefs and attitudes toward communication, emphasizing aspects such as respect, harmony, indirectness and balance.

WORDS ARE LIMITED

Chinese people believe that not everything can be expressed or described with words. In Chinese, we say:

言不尽意 yán bù jìn yì
"Not saying all that is felt."

只可意会，不可言传。 Zhǐ kě yì huì, bùkě yánchuán.
"Can be felt but can't be expressed in words."

These expressions reveal several insights. First, words are inherently limited, particularly in expressing one's feelings. Often, we find that words are insufficient and fail to convey the intended impact. In English, similar expressions exist to highlight this limitation, such as "Words cannot express how grateful I am for your help." Hence, we must often rely on other means of communication, such as body language. As successful communicators, we must learn to appreciate and understand the unspoken aspects of communication. This concept aligns closely with Hall's theory of high-context communication cultures, like China, where context significantly influences the intended meaning, not just the words themselves. The above expression underscores why Chinese communication relies heavily on nonverbal cues and context to fully grasp the conveyed message.

SAYING TOO MUCH IS TROUBLE

Not only do Chinese culture and idioms suggest that language has its limitations, but they also imply that excessive talking can be risky. These idioms demonstrate a preference for brevity over verbosity, and for silence over minimal speech. This does not imply that Chinese people are unfriendly or avoid small talk. Rather, historical events have ingrained in Chinese society the belief that listening is more valuable than speaking. This ethos encourages caution in communication, emphasizing the importance of being mindful about potentially revealing information unintentionally through speech.

> 祸从口出 huò cóng kǒu chū
> "Misfortune comes from the mouth."

> 言多必失 yán duō bì shī
> "He (she) who talks errs much."

> 沉默是金 chénmò shì jīn
> "Silence is gold."

The proverb 祸从口出 (huò cóng kǒu chū), translating to "misfortune comes from the mouth," dates back to the Jin Dynasty (266 – 420). It underscores the importance of thoughtful speech and the potential consequences of speaking without due consideration. Similarly, the proverb 言多必失 (yán duō bì shī), literally "too much talk is bound to fail," conveys that excessive talking, overconfidence or rashness can jeopardize success or lead to losses.

Both proverbs highlight the value of silence and caution, particularly in critical decision-making or significant occasions. They advocate for careful consideration before speaking, ensuring that one's words are precise, sensible and fitting for the context.

Furthermore, these proverbs reflect deeply rooted values in Chinese culture: modesty and prudence. These traits are highly regarded, especially in the context of significant decisions or facing crucial challenges. The proverb "too much talk will lead to loss" serves as a reminder, urging people to exercise restraint and caution in both speech and actions.

There are numerous stories in Chinese history that echo these beliefs. Allow me to share one such story with you.

During the Qing Dynasty, in Jimo County, there was a scholar named Zhang Sheng. In his younger days, he was frivolous and loved to crack jokes, often without considering the consequences. Recently, his wife had passed away. He wanted to remarry, so he sought the help of a matchmaker.

On his way to the matchmaker's house, Zhang Sheng happened to see the wife of the matchmaker's neighbour. He sneakily glanced at her a few times and found her to be very beautiful. Upon arriving at the matchmaker's residence, Zhang Sheng jokingly said to her, "I just saw your neighbour's wife, and she is both young and gorgeous. She would be the perfect match you could fine for me." The matchmaker, joining in the jest, replied, "Well, you'd have to kill her husband first, then I could arrange the match for you." Zhang Sheng laughed and said, "Alright, it's a deal."

A little over a month later, the matchmaker's neighbour went out to collect debts and was murdered in the suburbs. The county magistrate arrested the deceased's neighbours, torturing them to extract the truth of the incident, but no leads were found. Only the matchmaker revealed the jest she had shared with Zhang Sheng.

The county magistrate, suspecting Zhang Sheng's involvement, had him arrested. However, no matter how much he was questioned, Zhang Sheng would not admit to the murder. The magistrate also suspected that the deceased's wife was having an affair with Zhang Sheng, so she was arrested and subjected to all kinds of severe torture to extract a confession. Unable to bear the torment, the deceased's wife was forced to confess.

The county magistrate then interrogated Zhang Sheng again. Zhang Sheng said, "She is frail and cannot endure torture. Everything she said isn't true. She was wronged in the first place, and now you want to impose the crime of infidelity on her. Even if heaven doesn't show mercy to her, how can I stand by and watch her suffer? I am willing to confess the truth: I had originally planned to kill her husband and then take her as my wife. The murder was all my doing; she knew nothing about it."

The county magistrate pressed further, "Do you have any evidence?" Zhang Sheng replied, "I have the blood-stained clothes as proof." The magistrate sent people to search his house, but naturally, they found nothing. Zhang Sheng was then tortured further, being brought to the brink of death several times. He eventually said, "It's probably because my mother couldn't bear to produce the evidence that would seal my fate. Let me retrieve it myself." The magistrate then escorted Zhang Sheng back to his home to fetch the blood-stained clothes.

Once home, Zhang Sheng told his mother, "Quickly give me a blood-stained garment. Even if you don't, I will still die. Death is inevitable for me, so sooner would be better than later." Zhang's mother, in tears, went into an inner room. After a while, she emerged with a blood-stained garment and handed it to Zhang Sheng.

Upon careful examination, the county magistrate indeed found blood stains on the clothing and subsequently sentenced Zhang Sheng to death by beheading. During the second review of the case, Zhang Sheng had no different story to tell.

After half a year, the day of execution was drawing near. As the county magistrate was conducting the final review of the prisoners, a man suddenly stormed into the court, eyes burning with anger as he glared at the official. He shouted, "You're so incompetent and muddled; how can you govern the people!" Several bailiffs tried to apprehend him, but with a swing of his arm, they were all thrown to the ground.

Terrified, the county magistrate thought of escaping, but the man loudly proclaimed, "I am General Zhou from the presence of Lord Guan! If you, an inept official, dare to move, I will behead you on the spot!" The county magistrate trembled in fear, listening intently. The man continued, "The true murderer is Gong Biao. What does this have to do with Zhang Sheng!" After speaking, the man collapsed to the ground, appearing lifeless.

After a while, he regained consciousness, his face pale. When the crowd inquired about his identity, it turned out he was Gong Biao. The county magistrate then ordered him to be tortured for a confession, and Gong Biao fully admitted to his crimes.

It turned out that Gong Biao was a notorious troublemaker. When he learned that the matchmaker's neighbour was returning from debt collection, he figured there must be a significant sum of money in his pouch. Gong Biao murdered him, but to his disappointment, he found nothing of value. He later heard that Zhang Sheng had been tortured into a false confession and secretly felt relieved. But that day, he was drunk and when he arrived at the court, he had no recollection of his actions.

The county magistrate inquired about the origin of the blood-stained garment, but Zhang Sheng had no idea. When they summoned Zhang Sheng's mother and asked her, it was revealed that she had slashed her own arm to stain the clothing with blood. Upon examination, the scar on her left arm had not fully healed, causing the county magistrate great shock and dismay.

Subsequently, due to this miscarriage of justice, the county magistrate was impeached and removed from his post.

He was later punished for his misdeeds and died in prison. Over a year later, the neighbour's mother intended to marry off the widow. Out of gratitude for Zhang Sheng's noble sacrifice, the widow chose to marry him.

Fortunately for Zhang Sheng, he was free and married the widow of his dreams. However, if it wasn't because of his thoughtless joke, none of the people involved would have suffered so much.

Another key aspect of this belief is the importance of being brief and to the point in our communications, especially in urgent and critical situations. A famous story from Chinese history that embodies this principle is the story of Li Shizhong remonstrating with Taizong.

Li Shizhong, a minister in the Tang Dynasty, was deeply worried after seeing the struggle between Emperor Taizong Li Shimin and Prince Li Jiancheng. He got to know that Prince Li Jiancheng was secretly planning to rebel. He believed that this battle would not only lead to internal division and chaos in the Tang Dynasty, but also affect the development of the entire country. Therefore, he decided to advise Tang Taizong Li Shimin of this.

On 20 December, the first year of Chongzhen (that is, the first year of Chongzhen in Tang Dynasty), a secret attack was planned. At that time, Tang Taizong was drinking and having fun at a banquet. Li Shizhong advised Tang Taizong with a note. There were only eight Chinese characters written on this note, translated as: "Be careful not to believe him. Beware of him." Although Li Shizhong's sentence was short, it was concise and to the point, enough for Tang Taizong to understand what he meant.

After Tang Taizong saw the note, he attached great importance to it and immediately stopped the banquet and sent someone to investigate the matter. In the end, he discovered

Li Jiancheng and Li Yuanji's plot to rebel and killed them. Without Li Shizhong's advice, the Tang Dynasty might have been divided and perished due to internal divisions.

This story illustrates how concise and targeted communication can be sufficiently persuasive. Li Shizhong's words were few, but they were impactful. Thus, it's not only vital to have the courage to speak up, but also essential to use appropriate language and methods. This approach ensures that our contributions are well-founded and beneficial, effectively achieving the desired impact.

ONE MUST HONOUR ONE'S WORD

Integrity holds significant value in China, with ancient beliefs emphasizing the importance of keeping one's word in both personal and social contexts. Fulfilling promises is a respected virtue in personal and business relationships, closely linked to the Chinese concept of 诚信 (chéngxìn, honesty). This term comprises two characters: 诚 (chéng, sincerity), representing loyalty and honesty toward others, and 信 (xìn, faithfulness), signifying the quality of being trustworthy and keeping promises.

A profound expression underscoring the importance of this principle is the Chinese proverb "一言既出，驷马难追" (Yì yán jì chū, sì mǎ nán zhuī), translating to "A word spoken cannot be chased back even by a team of four horses." This proverb originates from an ancient Chinese narrative recorded in the Analects of Confucius 《论语·颜渊》, attributed to Zigong, a student of Confucius.

The story involves Jizi Cheng, a high official in the State of Wei, who questioned the necessity of literary grace for a person with good character. Zigong, countering this view, argued that both character and literary grace were essential for a gentleman, symbolizing both substance and style. He used the analogy of the irrevocability of spoken words, comparing them to a team of four horses, the fastest transportation of that era, to emphasize the irreversible nature of speech and the significance of cultural expression.

The phrase "一言既出，驷马难追" later evolved and appeared in a Yuan Dynasty drama by Li Shouqing, depicting the story of Wu Zixu seeking revenge for his father. This idiom encapsulates the wisdom that once words are spoken, their impact is as swift and uncontainable as a chariot driven by four horses, a symbol of speed and irreversibility in ancient China. It serves as a timeless reminder to speak thoughtfully, considering the enduring impact of our words.

Therefore, it should no longer be surprising that the Chinese communication style often leans toward being indirect and ambiguous. This approach provides a measure of protection and flexibility for the speaker. In the event of changing circumstances, their integrity or credibility is less likely to be called into question.

THE ART OF LISTENING

In the previous section, we explored beliefs about communication from the perspective of the speaker. Now, let's shift our focus to the listener. Given that speakers are encouraged to be mindful of their speech, often expressing themselves in an indirect and ambiguous manner, it necessitates a certain level of skill and awareness from the listener to facilitate effective communication.

HOW SHOULD ONE LISTEN

The Chinese perspective on listening is encapsulated in the idiom '察言观色' (Cháyánguānsè), which implies that while paying attention to what is said is important, observing how it is said is even more crucial. This concept is further illustrated in the Chinese character for 'listen,' 听 (tīng), in its traditional form, which offers profound insight into the cultural understanding of listening in China.

The character, in its traditional form, comprises several parts:

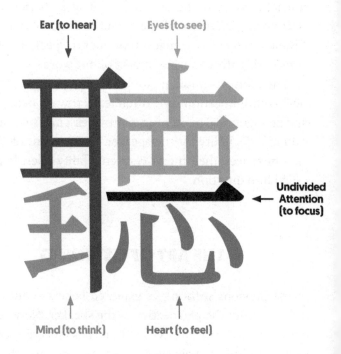

THE TRADITIONAL CHINESE CHARACTER OF 'LISTEN'

- **Ear (耳):** This represents the basic act of hearing with one's ears, the fundamental sensory input in listening.

- **King (王):** This element suggests the respect and attention that should be accorded when listening, akin to the attentiveness expected in the presence of a king.

- **Ten (十) and Eye (目):** Together, these signify that effective listening involves not just auditory but also visual observation and attention to detail.

- **Heart (心):** Arguably the most essential component, it implies that true listening is not solely an auditory or intellectual task, but also involves empathy, understanding and emotional engagement.

The composition of 听 highlights a holistic approach to listening. It's not merely about hearing words, but involves interpreting and understanding them within a broader context, which includes nonverbal cues and emotional resonance. This comprehensive view of listening in Chinese culture underscores the importance of active and empathetic communication, necessitating full engagement in the process of listening.

Indeed, it appears that the Chinese conceptualization of 'active listening' was established thousands of years ago. This is particularly impressive, but it also seems to stem from the nuanced communication styles inherent in Chinese culture, which require a high level of listening and observational skills.

THE POWER OF
LISTENING MINDFULLY

Let's explore another expression that underscores the opportunities and positive outcomes derived from careful listening. The saying "说者无意，听者有心" (shuō zhě wú yì, tīng zhě yǒu xīn) translates to "the speaker has no intention, the listener has intention." This adage suggests that a perceptive listener can glean valuable information from both what is said and how it is said, often to their advantage. It highlights the importance of being a mindful listener, capable of discerning truths that the speaker may unconsciously reveal. Thus, this expression emphasizes the skill of listening not just for the spoken words but for the underlying messages and intentions.

At a discourse level, it usually indicates that one discloses news that may be taken advantage of by another person or news that may cause negative effects. Let's read another Chinese story.

> It is said that Liu Bang and Xiang Yu, two notable figures in Chinese history, were classmates in their youth. Xiang Yu, known for not getting along well with his peers, once faced a particularly distressing situation.
>
> After being bullied one day, Xiang Yu, feeling deeply wronged, ran to the beach and cried from day into night, refusing to cease. During the night, an old man with a white beard approached him. Comforting Xiang Yu, the old man said, "You are destined for great things, and this bullying is but a temporary setback. Return here in three nights, and I will bestow upon you a treasure that will make the world yours."
>
> The next day, after being bullied again, Xiang Yu, in his anger, warned his tormentors, "Beware, for when I rule the world, I shall not spare you." His peers, thinking he was fabricating stories, mocked him. In an attempt to prove his truth,

Xiang Yu recounted his encounter with the old man. However, this only led to further ridicule. Unbeknownst to them, Liu Bang was listening intently and remembered the tale.

On the third night, Liu Bang stealthily went to the beach. The old man arrived, and in the darkness, mistaking Liu Bang for Xiang Yu, handed him a 'Dragon Slaying Sword.' He instructed Liu Bang, "When you grow up, if a white snake blocks your path near Mangyang Village, use this sword to slay it. Then lead your army to seize Xianyang, and the world will be yours." Delighted, Liu Bang thanked the old man and left with the sword.

As history unfolded, Liu Bang indeed used the 'Dragon Slaying Sword' to kill a white snake, captured Xianyang City, and ultimately founded the Han Dynasty. The tale thus illustrates how Xiang Yu's inadvertent revelation of the secret, which was disregarded by others, was astutely heeded by Liu Bang, leading him to his eventual conquest of the world.

For those who know Chinese history, you will know this story is not real and it is definitely not how Liu Bang got the world and established Han Dynasty. But the essence is there. Xiang Yu gave out key information without thinking about it. Liu Bang, on the other hand, took advantage of it and used it to his gain.

LISTENING FOR INTERTEXTUALITY

The phrase "言外之意" (yán wài zhī yì), translating to "more is meant than meets the ear," shows the importance of discerning unspoken or implied meanings in communication. This highlights the high-context nature of Chinese communication, where the unsaid can be as significant as what is spoken. Such communication relies heavily on shared cultural and contextual understanding among the parties involved.

In Chinese culture, '言外之意,' akin to the concept of 'intertextuality,' often refers to the true intention or meaning beneath the surface of words. Chinese people typically grasp the underlying message by observing the speaker's expressions, tone and behaviour. For instance, if someone says "It's all right" with a hesitant tone and unnatural expression, it might indicate an unspoken concern or issue. Thus, it becomes crucial to pay attention to nonverbal cues like tone, facial expressions and body language to truly understand the intended message.

This skill of reading between the lines is particularly vital in Chinese business and political communications. Given the frequent use of implicit and euphemistic language, interpreting the speaker's true intentions through nonverbal cues is key. In business negotiations, this understanding can lead to more beneficial cooperation by better comprehending the other party's needs and interests. Similarly, in political communication, it enables a deeper grasp of international relations and foreign policy nuances.

Overall, these concepts highlight the negotiable nature of communication in Chinese culture. Meaning is derived not only from words but also from context, the relationship between the speaker and listener, and the nuanced, unspoken elements. This dynamic necessitates a heightened awareness and sensitivity to the subtleties of language and interaction, thereby shaping a distinctive communication style deeply rooted in Chinese society.

SUMMARY

In this chapter, I shared some beliefs Chinese people hold regarding communication. This explains the 'why' of Chinese communication. Chinese communication beliefs, as evidenced through the rich tapestry of its idioms, present a nuanced and profound perspective on human interaction. At the core of this ancient culture's philosophy on communication are four principal tenets:

- **Language is Limited:** Chinese idioms stress that while language is a powerful tool, it has limitations. Overelaboration or verbosity can sometimes obscure the intended message. Simplicity and clarity are often more effective than an overabundance of words.
- **The Gravity of Words:** Words aren't mere transient sounds; they carry weight and consequence. The Chinese ethos emphasizes the importance of speaking with intention and caution, understanding that once spoken, words hold the speaker to their implications and potential outcomes.
- **Cocreation of Meaning:** Communication isn't a one-sided activity where the speaker holds all responsibility for conveying a message. Instead, it's a shared venture. The listener, too, plays an active role in deducing and deriving meaning, often diving into subtext and reading between the lines.
- **Holistic Listening:** True understanding doesn't stem from merely hearing words. It requires active, comprehensive listening – capturing tone, observing nonverbal cues, understanding context and sensing the emotions that accompany the spoken words.

For anyone aiming to engage with this culture, understanding these principles is paramount. It's a reminder that
in the dance of communication, every step, gesture and
pause holds significance. Through its idioms and beliefs,
Chinese culture offers a masterclass on communication –
encouraging thoughtfulness, mutual respect and a deeper,
holistic understanding.

CHAPTER 7

Chinese Cultural Values

We are now peeling away another layer of the onion and getting to the core of understanding any culture: cultural values. These can be defined as the shared beliefs, norms, attitudes and expectations that guide and influence the behaviour of individuals within a specific cultural group. These values shape how people perceive the world, interact with others and make decisions. Cultural values can be influenced by factors such as history, religion, geography and social dynamics within a community (Schwartz, 1999).

In this chapter, let's foster understanding about what Chinese core values are, how they are formed and how they influence Chinese communication. We will cover three must-know philosophical influences: 1. Confucianism; 2. Taoism; and 3. Buddhism. By recognizing and appreciating the Chinese cultural values, you can develop greater cultural competence, empathy and adaptability when communicating with China.

CONFUCIANISM: THE COMPASS OF COMMUNICATION IN ASIA

Imagine a philosophy acting as a compass, guiding an entire civilization in its communication, connection and community practices. For many Asian countries, particularly China and Korea, this guiding force is Confucianism. Its influence extends beyond religious or cultural rites, profoundly shaping the essence of social interactions.

Confucius, or Kongzi (孔子) and Kong Fuzi (孔夫子) in Chinese, was a pivotal philosopher, teacher and politician during China's Spring and Autumn period. Born in the state of Lu (today's Qufu, Shandong Province), he stands as one of the most influential thinkers in Chinese culture, mainly due to his teachings and the philosophy that later became known as Confucianism.

Confucius advocated for personal and societal harmony through the cultivation of moral virtues and adherence to social rituals. He stressed the significance of education and self-improvement, urging individuals to pursue moral excellence and righteousness. His teachings offered practical guidance for daily life, emphasizing ethical behaviour, relationships and social order.

FIVE BASIC CONCEPTS

Now, let's explore some of Confucius's key teachings and understand how they influence Chinese communication. The fundamental tenets of Confucianism can be encapsulated in the concepts of Ren (仁, benevolence), Li (礼, propriety), Xiao (孝, filial piety), Yi (义, righteousness) and Zhong (忠, loyalty).

Ren (仁): Benevolence or Humaneness

Ren, often translated as 'benevolence' or 'humaneness,' stands at the heart of Confucianism. It is a principle that underscores treating others with kindness and empathy. As Confucius stated, "仁者爱人" (Rénzhě ài rén), which means "the benevolent love of others" (Analects 12:22). This tenet has led Chinese people to place a high value on harmonious interpersonal relationships, thereby fostering a collectivist culture.

In the realm of communication, Ren advocates for empathy, kindness and consideration toward others. It encourages sensitivity to the feelings of others, aiming to prevent discomfort or embarrassment. This perspective underpins the preference for an indirect communication style, especially in situations that could lead to someone 'losing face.' Indirect communication is, therefore, often employed in scenarios where directness might cause unease or social tension.

Li (礼): Rituals or Etiquette

Li encompasses the rituals, customs and etiquette fundamental to social behaviour. Confucius championed the practice of Li as a means of cultivating moral character and maintaining social harmony. A notable maxim from the Book of Rites, "(礼记), '礼之用，和为贵" (Lǐ zhī yòng, hé wéi guì), suggests that the ultimate aim of Li is to achieve harmony. In Chinese society, adherence to Li determines appropriate conduct across various contexts, evident in the emphasis on social hierarchy, respect for elders, and reverence for authority.

This understanding lays the philosophical foundation for the hierarchical structure of Chinese social order. Li necessitates compliance with proper etiquette, rituals and social norms in communication, influencing various facets of Chinese life.

For instance, during a wedding, a Chinese guest would adhere to traditional etiquette, such as presenting a red envelope of money as a gift and dressing appropriately to honour the couple and their families. At the wedding banquet, proposing a toast to the bride and groom is a part of the ritualistic practice.

Moreover, Li influences how Chinese people adhere to established norms in communication, showing respect and deference based on social status. In formal encounters, addressing individuals with their full title and surname (e.g., Director Wang or Professor Li) is a norm, signifying respect for their position. A handshake may be accompanied by a slight bow, reflecting deference to the person's status. Similarly, seating arrangements in business meetings or dining settings are meticulously considered to reflect appropriate respect and status.

In the previous chapter, we discussed a key characteristic of Chinese communication style identified by Gao and Ting-Toomey, known as 听话 (listening-centeredness). An essential aspect of this style is the unequal right to speak, wherein speaking in Chinese culture follows its own set of etiquettes. Behaviours such as 插嘴 (interrupting) or 还口 (talking back) are deemed disrespectful or impolite, particularly in hierarchical contexts.

Xiao (孝): Filial Piety

Filial piety, a cornerstone of Confucianism, underscores the respect and loyalty children owe their parents. As Confucius stated, "孝顺为先" (Xiàoshùn wéi xiān), meaning "filial piety comes first" (Analects 1:6). This principle has significantly shaped the Chinese family structure, highlighting duties and responsibilities within the family, such as caring for elderly parents, continuing the family lineage and upholding the family's honour.

In Chinese culture, the family unit is regarded as the bedrock of society, tasked with nurturing children and passing down cultural traditions and values. Children are instilled with the values of honouring their parents and elders and maintaining the family's reputation. *Guanxi*, another crucial concept in Chinese culture, refers to the network of personal relationships and social connections. Family relationships are seen as the most vital and influential *guanxi*, implying that strong family ties often lead to better access to opportunities and resources. This concept will be elaborated upon in the next chapter.

Additionally, Chinese culture places significant emphasis on collectivism over individualism. The family's needs often take precedence over individual desires, with family members expected to support each other, especially in times of need.

During family meals, it is common for younger members to serve their grandparents and parents first, demonstrating respect by waiting for elders to begin eating. Polite language and deferential behaviour toward elders are also customary, reflecting deep-seated values of respect. These principles extend into the business realm as well.

The family name, or surname, holds great importance in Chinese identity, passed down through generations. Many Chinese families take immense pride in their ancestral history and genealogy. Consequently, a prevalent practice in addressing individuals combines the person's surname with their job title, such as 'Xiang, Dr' in formal contexts. Adhering to this method of address with Chinese colleagues and clients, particularly in formal settings, is usually well-received and appreciated.

The importance of family ties in Chinese culture extends to close friends, who are often regarded as 'brothers' or 'sisters.' This reflects the story in Chapter 1, where 'brothers' are used to address clients or managers, reinforcing the relationship and the obligations it entails.

Yi (义): Righteousness

Yi (义), or righteousness, denotes the moral inclination to do good, acting with integrity and justice. As Confucius said, "君子义以为质" (Jūnzǐ yì yǐ wéi zhì), which means "a gentleman takes righteousness as his substance" (Analects 4:16). Yi has influenced Chinese society by cultivating a sense of justice and emphasizing moral principles in decision-making.

In communication, this principle manifests through honest and forthright interactions, especially among close friends or insiders. For instance, a Chinese person may offer candid advice in difficult situations, valuing truth and justice over mere agreement to maintain harmony. This direct approach in advice-giving is not only a sign of insider communication but also an expression of Yi, defining the qualities of a good friend. Consequently, honesty and directness become justifiable and proper.

Yi also influences fairness in interactions. It explains why, in business negotiations, a Chinese businessperson may prioritize long-term, mutually beneficial relationships over short-term gains, valuing trust and considering their counterparts as 'friends.'

Zhong (忠): Loyalty

Zhong (忠), or loyalty, pertains to the devotion and commitment one shows toward their ruler, family and friends. Confucius stated, "忠言逆耳" (Zhōngyán nì'ěr), meaning "loyal words are often unpleasant to the ear" (Analects 1:14). This principle encourages honesty and loyalty, even in challenging circumstances.

In communication, Zhong promotes commitment and honesty toward family, friends and superiors. In the workplace, for instance, a Chinese employee may not openly criticize their boss, instead opting to voice concerns privately, showing loyalty and respect. Demonstrating loyalty may involve diligent work, being a dependable team member, supporting colleagues and fostering collaboration.

The above five concepts have guilded Chinese people for centuries. According to Chinese scholar Chen (1997), these principles are not merely suggestions but the rules governing human behaviour in society. They define the concept of 君子, the ideal or superior person, providing standards for morally commendable actions.

UNDERSTANDING CONFUCIAN THOUGHT ON RELATIONSHIPS AND COMMUNICATION IN CHINESE BUSINESS

In the previous section, we examined how Confucianism, an ancient Chinese philosophical system, emphasizes the sanctity of human relationships. It advocates understanding one's role and fulfilling it diligently, akin to an actor in a theatrical performance.

Confucius highlighted the significance of addressing terms within relationships. For example, in a Chinese family, one wouldn't call their uncle "Peter" but rather "Uncle," with the Chinese language providing specific terms indicating gender, and whether the relative is from the mother's or father's side. This intricate family tree illustrates the roles and responsibilities a Chinese child learns to navigate.

Chinese Family Tree and Address of Terms

Understanding one's role (or 'address of term') dictates the expected behaviour. Hagemann (1986) aptly describes it thus: "Recognizing one's 'name' instinctively guides appropriate attitudes and actions, much like adopting a character in a play." Within Chinese family, you don't call your uncle 'Peter,' you call them 'Uncle.' The Chinese language can clearly indicate their gender, whether they are on your mother or father's side, and their relation to your parents. This is what a Chinese family tree looks like and what a Chinese child needs to learn to about addressing their relatives.

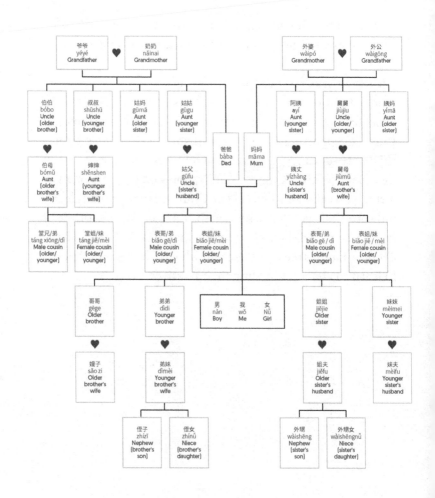

CHINESE FAMILY TREE AND ADDRESS OF TERMS

This principle significantly influences business communication. Before discussions commence, participants establish their relationships through 'titles,' setting the stage for the interaction. Titles reveal not only technical aspects but, importantly, managerial positions, indicating an individual's status and responsibilities. This understanding is crucial in negotiations, as it clarifies whom one is negotiating with.

Modesty also plays a vital role. Confucius taught that true gentlemen express morality through modesty. In Chinese culture, self-deprecation, even to the point of underplaying one's achievements, is a mark of integrity. For example, an expert might modestly respond to praise by downplaying their knowledge. This reflects cultural humility rather than ignorance.

In dialogue, Chinese communicators often minimize their own standing and elevate that of their counterparts. Describing oneself with terms like "your younger brother" is not self-deprecation but a recognition of one's societal or business position.

In one study, Nie (2003) examined a range of Chinese business correspondences. In a resignation letter addressed to his department director, the person who resigned immediately positioned himself as subordinate by referring to himself as "this humble subordinate." This approach set the stage for him to fulfil his role with due respect and gratitude. He expressed deep appreciation for the director's guidance, likening it to being sheltered by a "giant tree" and vowing to remember this kindness for life.

> This humble subordinate, sheltered in the past 20 years by your honoured giant tree [meaning he was protected by the director], always benefits from your instructions, so this humble subordinate will never forget your kindness until all my teeth are decayed [meaning until he dies.] [p. 167]

This method of communication serves two key purposes in the Chinese business context. First, it establishes a clear hierarchy and relationship dynamics, such as the inferior-to-superior relationship between the Chinese employee and his director. Second, it lays a moral foundation for interactions, showcasing one's integrity and worthiness of trust and cooperation. By adhering to these role-defined expectations of respect and consideration, individuals like the person who resigned effectively cement harmonious and smooth business relationships.

As we can see, for Chinese people, by positioning oneself as modest and showing respect, one effectively garners trust and establishes credibility. While Western cultures might extol the virtues of self-expression and individuality, Chinese culture views the self as a cog in a vast machinery of relationships. In both personal and business arenas, this relational approach shapes interactions, guiding individuals to prioritize harmony, respect and collective success over individual acclaim.

Confucian Views on Profits and Personal Gain

Now, we turn to the Confucian perspective on personal gain, emphasizing that virtue and righteousness should supersede the desire for profit. This philosophy views gains through unrighteous means as ephemeral and lacking substance.

Confucian teachings advocate modesty, not only in material gains but also in seeking fame or excessive praise. Profits aligned with righteousness, benefiting society or collective groups, are deemed acceptable. However, with China's shift to a market-driven economy, perceptions have changed. While personal achievements are increasingly valued, they are approached with a nod to cultural norms.

The emergence of 'Confucian consumerism' marries traditional values with modern economic behaviours. This approach allows personal profit-seeking, provided it maintains societal harmony and adheres to Li, or proper conduct.

In summary, while Confucianism traditionally disdains the selfish pursuit of personal profits, it recognizes the need for gains that contribute to societal well-being. This balance between individual ambition and collective good remains a cornerstone of Chinese culture, persisting even as modern China evolves.

TAOISM – THE WAY

Laozi, also spelled Lao Tzu or Lao-Tze, is a legendary figure in Chinese philosophy, credited as the founder of Taoism. He is believed to have lived around the 6th century BCE, although there is considerable debate about the exact details of his life. Laozi is said to be the author of the foundational Taoist text, the *Tao Te Ching* (道德经), which presents the essential principles of Taoism, focusing on the concept of the Tao (道), meaning 'the Way.'

Taoism has been influential in Chinese culture for several reasons:

- **Emphasis on Harmony with Nature:** Taoism stresses the importance of living in harmony with the natural world and embracing the interconnectedness of all things. This principle has profoundly influenced Chinese culture, shaping traditional beliefs about the environment, medicine and agriculture.

- **The Concept of Wu Wei (无为):** Wu Wei, often translated as 'nonaction' or 'effortless action,' is a central Taoist concept that encourages individuals to act in accordance with the natural flow of life. This idea has permeated various aspects of Chinese society, promoting a balanced and adaptable approach to problem-solving and decision-making.

- **Integration with Chinese Religion and Folklore:** Over time, Taoism has become intertwined with Chinese religion and folklore, giving rise to a rich tapestry of myths, legends and rituals. Many of the deities, immortals and spiritual beings revered in Chinese culture have roots in Taoist beliefs, adding to the philosophy's influence.

- **Influence on Chinese Art and Aesthetics:** Taoist principles have inspired Chinese art and aesthetics, particularly in the areas of painting, calligraphy and poetry. The focus on harmony with nature, balance and simplicity has guided artists in their creative pursuits, resulting in a unique and enduring artistic tradition.

- **Complementarity with Confucianism:** Although Taoism and Confucianism differ in their focus and approach, they have coexisted and complemented each other throughout Chinese history. While Confucianism emphasizes social order, hierarchy and morality, Taoism provides a more individualistic, introspective and spiritual perspective. This balance of ideas has helped shape Chinese culture and thought.

   While Laozi's *Tao Te Ching* does not explicitly discuss communication in the same way Confucian texts do, the philosophy of Taoism does provide principles that influence communication styles in Chinese culture. Here are some Taoist concepts with their original Chinese text, detailed explanations and real-life examples of how they impact communication.

- **Wu Wei (无为) in Communication:** Wu Wei, often translated as 'nonaction' or 'effortless action,' is a central concept in Taoism. Chapter 63 of the *Tao Te Ching* says:

   > 为无为，事无事，味无味。(Chapter 63)
   > (Wéi wú wéi, shì wú shì, wèi wú wèi.)
   > "Practice nonaction. Work without doing. Taste the tasteless."

Wu Wei suggests that one should act naturally, in accordance with the flow of life. In communication, this might mean allowing conversations to unfold organically, listening attentively, and responding with authenticity and spontaneity. In a business negotiation, a Taoist-influenced person might remain patient and observant, allowing the conversation to develop naturally rather than pushing aggressively for their own interests. They might also adapt their communication style to the situation, seeking to maintain harmony and balance throughout the discussion.

Wu Wei can mean being sensitive to the context, adapting to the situation and not forcing one's opinions on others. In a group discussion, a Taoist-inspired communicator might listen attentively to others' opinions, speak when it feels natural, and refrain from dominating the conversation or interrupting others. This allows for a more open and harmonious exchange of ideas.

- **Emphasis on Balance (阴阳) and Harmony (和谐):** The Taoist concept of Yin and Yang (阴阳) represents the balance between opposing forces in nature. This idea can be applied to communication, where the balance between speaking and listening, expressing and receiving, is essential for achieving harmony.

  The *Tao Te Ching* states:

  上善若水。水善利萬物而不爭，處衆人之所惡，故幾於道。
  (Chapter 8)
  (Shàng shàn ruò shuǐ. Shuǐ shàn lì wàn wù ér bù zhēng, chǔ zhòng rén zhī suǒ wù, gù jī yú dào.)
  "The highest good is like water. Water gives life to ten thousand things and does not strive. It flows in places men reject and so is like the Tao."

This passage highlights the importance of being adaptable and harmonious, like water, which benefits all things without competing with them. In communication, this principle may inspire individuals to be flexible, open-minded and cooperative, seeking consensus and mutual understanding. Although harmony is a key concept in Confucianism, the rationale and approach to achieving harmony is different. Confucius proposes social order and the obedience of such hierarchy. Whereas the rational of Laozi to achieve harmony is to follow the way nature is. Keeping good balance and being adaptable is how to achieve harmony.

When discussing a contentious issue, a person influenced by Taoism might strive to find common ground and build consensus rather than engage in heated arguments or impose their views on others. In a negotiation, a person influenced by Taoist principles might strive for balance in the discussion, ensuring that both parties have an equal opportunity to express their needs and concerns. They may also seek a harmonious outcome, where both sides feel satisfied and respected.

- **Appreciation for Simplicity (简约) and Naturalness (自然):** Taoism values simplicity and naturalness, encouraging individuals to be genuine and avoid pretence or extravagance in their actions and speech.

  The *Tao Te Ching* says:

  道可道，非常道。名可名，非常名。(Chapter 1)
  (Dào kě dào, fēi cháng dào. Míng kě míng, fēi cháng míng.)
  "The Tao that can be told is not the eternal Tao. The name that can be named is not the eternal name."

This passage suggests that the ultimate truth cannot be fully expressed through language, emphasizing the limitations of words. This explains the Chinese belief on the limitation of language and verbal communication.

When writing an email, a person following Taoist principles might use simple, clear language to convey their message, avoiding overly complex expressions or jargon. They may also be genuine and sincere in their tone, expressing their thoughts without exaggeration or deception.

- **The Importance of Humility (谦逊):** Like Confucianism, Taoism teaches the virtue of humility, emphasizing the importance of recognizing one's limitations and not boasting about one's achievements or abilities.

  In a job interview, a Taoist-inspired candidate might honestly share their skills and experiences without exaggerating their accomplishments. They might also show a willingness to learn from others and acknowledge areas where they can improve, demonstrating humility and self-awareness.

In conclusion, although Laozi's *Tao Te Ching* does not explicitly address communication, the philosophy of Taoism offers valuable principles that influence communication styles in Chinese culture. Concepts like Wu Wei, balance and harmony, simplicity and naturalness, and humility can provide guidance for more authentic, harmonious and effective communication.

BUDDHISM

Buddhism, originating in India, was introduced to China around the 1st or 2nd century CE and has since had a profound impact on Chinese culture and society. It has shaped various aspects of Chinese life, including philosophy, religion, art, literature and architecture.

Upon its arrival in China, Buddhism interacted with native Chinese philosophies like Confucianism and Taoism. Over time, these interactions led to the development of unique schools of Buddhist thought, such as Chan (Zen) Buddhism, Pure Land Buddhism and Tiantai Buddhism. These schools synthesized elements of native Chinese thought with Buddhist teachings, making Buddhism more relatable and accessible to the Chinese population.

Obviously, Buddhism is complex, but there are two key concepts that have great influence on Chinese society. These values are similar to Confucianism, which make them more easily integrated and accepted in Chinese society.

Buddhism teaches that actions have consequences (karma) and that these consequences can carry over into future lives through the process of rebirth. One's actions in the present life determine the conditions of the next life, and the cycle of birth and death (samsara) continues until one attains enlightenment and liberation (nirvana). This concept is very easily accepted by Chinese due to the key idea of reciprocity of the Confucius teaching. This reinforces the belief that keeping a positive relationship builds on continuous favours to strengthening the positive relationship and your personal network.

The other key Buddhism value is compassion, or the wish to alleviate the suffering of others. Compassionate communication involves understanding and empathizing with others, speaking in ways that foster connection and understanding. This is very similar to the concept of 仁

(benevolence or humaneness). Buddhism also teaches that all beings are interconnected and interdependent, emphasizing the importance of harmony and cooperation. This principle can foster a sense of connection and mutual respect in communication, encouraging individuals to consider the impact of their words and actions on others. We can see here the similarity to both Confucianism and Taoism.

Case Study –
Negotiation, Chinese Style

These shared principles among Confucianism, Taoism and Buddhism have contributed to shaping Chinese communication and politeness in society. The emphasis on harmony, the value of relationships, moral and ethical conduct, and mindfulness and self-cultivation have fostered communication styles that are respectful, considerate, empathetic, and focused on maintaining face and social harmony. At the same time, it also means that the Chinese decision-making process tends to be complex and dynamic as they may shift emphasis, subject to their current situation.

Background of the study: The research done by Tong Fang in 2006 confirms the combination of Chinese philosophical foundations underpinning the negotiation style of Chinese businesses. Tony Fang examines the unique dynamics of Sino-Western business negotiations. This study, grounded in a conceptual approach informed by personal interviews, offers insightful perspectives for Western businesses engaged in large industrial projects with Chinese counterparts.

Key findings: Fang identifies the Chinese negotiating style as a fluid blend of three distinct roles: "Maoist bureaucrat in learning," "Confucian gentleman" and "Sun Tzu-like strategist." This amalgamation reflects a deeper cultural foundation, notably the balance of Yin Yang thinking from Taoism, allowing Chinese negotiators to adapt their strategies based on the level of trust with their negotiating partners. He underscores that these styles are not static; they are responsive to the evolving political, cultural and strategic landscapes in China.

The study identifies key characteristics of each role:

1. Maoist Bureaucrat: This role aligns with governmental plans, prioritizing national interests and intertwining politics with business.
2. Confucian Gentleman: Here, the focus is on mutual trust, seeking win-win solutions, valuing righteousness over profit and favouring relationship-building over legalistic negotiations.
3. Sun Tzu-like Strategist: This role views negotiation as a zero-sum game, employing a variety of stratagems and psychological tactics to achieve objectives.

Implications: Chinese negotiation strategy combines Confucian cooperative approaches with Sun Tzu-like competitive strategies. The choice between cooperation and competition hinges on the level of trust established between negotiating parties. In order to be successful in negotiating with Chinese, knowing the philosophical influence and staying flexible is key.

SUMMARY

Confucianism, Taoism and Buddhism, while distinct in their teachings and philosophies, share several core principles that have profoundly shaped communication and politeness in Chinese society. Key similarities include:

Emphasis on Harmony: These philosophies collectively value harmony – social harmony in Confucianism, harmony with nature in Taoism and inner harmony in Buddhism. This unified focus significantly influences Chinese communication, encouraging politeness, indirectness and the preservation of face in social interactions.

Valuing Relationships: The importance of relationships is a central theme in all three teachings. Confucianism discusses 'Li' (ritual propriety) and the Five Cardinal Relationships, Taoism highlights the interconnectedness of all beings, and Buddhism advocates for compassion and loving-kindness. This emphasis fosters respectful, considerate and empathetic communication, acknowledging one's role and duties in various social contexts.

Moral and Ethical Conduct: Each philosophy underscores the importance of moral and ethical behaviour. Confucianism focuses on virtue cultivation, Taoism on living in accord with the Tao, and Buddhism on adhering to the Noble Eightfold Path. These shared ethical values promote a communication style that is respectful, honest and kind.

Mindfulness and Self-Cultivation: Taoism and Buddhism strongly advocate mindfulness and self-cultivation, including meditation and self-reflection. While not explicitly mentioned in Confucianism, self-cultivation is integral to becoming a Junzi (a morally upright person). This emphasis encourages attentiveness and understanding in interactions, enhancing empathy and connection.

Gaining insight into these philosophical and cultural values can significantly enhance your understanding of those you interact with in Chinese society. While this chapter provides an overview, there is much more to explore in the vast 'iceberg' of Chinese culture and philosophy, such as Sun Tzu, the great strategist. Investing time to read on such subjects is highly encouraged for a more comprehensive understanding.

Key Chinese Cultural Words

In this chapter, we discuss the concept of cultural keywords, as introduced by Anna Wierzbicka in 1997, to understand communication and behaviours within the Chinese context. Cultural keywords are unique to each culture, embodying deep meanings and values that reflect the core beliefs, norms and values of a society. This exploration not only deepens our comprehension of different cultures but also aids in navigating the intricacies of intercultural communication more effectively.

Drawing from Wierzbicka's seminal work, *Understanding Cultures through their Key Words: English, Russian, Polish, German and Japanese*, we gain a foundational understanding of how specific words in various languages are laden with significant cultural connotations. Building upon this framework, we will explore key Chinese cultural words such as 人情 (rénqíng), 关系 (guānxì), and 面子 (miànzi). These terms are pivotal in comprehending the nuances of Chinese social and business etiquette, offering a window into the subtleties of Chinese culture and communication.

Through this analysis, we aim to illuminate the underlying cultural underpinnings that shape interactions and behaviours in Chinese society, enhancing our capability to engage more meaningfully and respectfully in a cross-cultural context.

DEFINING CULTURAL KEYWORDS

Cultural keywords, also known as key cultural concepts, are words or phrases that hold particular significance, meaning and value within a specific cultural context. These keywords often reflect the core values, beliefs and norms of a culture and can provide valuable insights into the underlying assumptions and thought patterns of a cultural group.

In her book *Understanding Cultures through their Key Words: English, Russian, Polish, German and Japanese*, Anna Wierzbicka (1997) explores the cultural significance of key words in these five languages. She examines how these keywords reveal insights into the core values and beliefs of each culture. Here are some examples of her findings for each language:

- **English**
  Privacy: This keyword highlights the importance of individual autonomy and personal boundaries in Anglophone cultures. It reflects the value placed on personal space and the right to control one's environment.

  Fairness: This term represents the emphasis on justice, equality and impartial treatment within English-speaking cultures. It underscores the importance of treating people fairly and without bias.

- **Russian**
  Dusha (душа): This term translates to 'soul' in English but carries deeper cultural significance in Russian. It represents the emotional, spiritual and moral aspects of a person and is often used to describe someone's character, feelings or the depth of their relationships.

Toska (тоска): A uniquely Russian word that encapsulates a deep sense of longing, melancholy or nostalgia. It reflects the Russian cultural penchant for introspection and emotional intensity.

- **Polish**
  Solidarność: Meaning 'solidarity,' this term played a crucial role in the Polish labour movement during the 1980s. It signifies unity, mutual support and the collective struggle for a common cause, reflecting the importance of community and shared goals in Polish culture.

  Rodzina: Translating to 'family,' this keyword emphasizes the strong value placed on family ties, loyalty and connectedness in Polish society.

- **German**
  Gemütlichkeit: This term embodies a sense of warmth, comfort and coziness often associated with social gatherings in German culture. It reflects the importance of creating a welcoming, relaxed atmosphere where people can enjoy each other's company.

  Ordnung: Meaning 'order,' this keyword highlights the value placed on structure, organization and rules in German society. It signifies the importance of maintaining orderliness and adhering to established norms.

- **Japanese**
  Wa (和): This term represents harmony, balance and the pursuit of peaceful coexistence in Japanese culture. It underlines the importance of maintaining harmonious relationships and avoiding conflict.

Giri (義理): Referring to social obligation or duty, this keyword demonstrates the significance of fulfilling one's responsibilities to others in Japanese society. It emphasizes loyalty, commitment and the importance of upholding social norms.

Wierzbicka's exploration of these cultural keywords sheds light on the values and beliefs that underpin each culture, helping to deepen our understanding of intercultural communication and enhance our ability to navigate cultural differences effectively. You may not speak all these languages, but you may have interacted with people who are native speakers of these languages.

CHINESE CULTURAL KEY WORDS

Now let's return to Chinese culture and some of its own keywords.

人情

Renqing (人情): This term embodies the concept of social obligation, favour and indebtedness in Chinese society. It highlights the importance of mutual assistance, reciprocity and fulfilling one's social responsibilities to maintain harmonious relationships. For this reason, it's a subtle yet powerful force that influences the way Chinese people communicate and engage with one another.

In the Chinese language, 欠人情 (qiàn rénqíng), 送人情 (sòng rénqíng) and 还人情 (huán rénqíng) are the three most common Chinese expressions that revolve around the concept of 'renqing' (人情), which emphasizes social obligations, favours and indebtedness in Chinese culture. Let's explore these expressions and their meanings:

- 欠人情 (qiàn rénqíng): Literally translated as "owing someone a favour," this phrase indicates that someone has received help or support from another person and, as a result, is indebted to them. In Chinese culture, it's important to maintain balanced relationships, so the person who owes the favour is expected to repay it in the future, either through a similar act of assistance or another gesture that demonstrates gratitude and appreciation. Therefore, most people would not be in a position of 欠人情.

- 送人情 (sòng rénqíng): This phrase translates to "giving a favour" or "offering goodwill." It refers to the act of voluntarily helping or supporting someone without any immediate expectation of repayment. This is a very ideal position to be in, as it shows the resourcefulness of the person. In addition, by offering assistance, the person giving the favor is demonstrating their willingness to establish or strengthen a relationship based on trust and reciprocity. The recipient of the favour, in turn, is expected to remember this gesture and be willing to repay it when the opportunity arises.

- 还人情 (huán rénqíng): Translated as "returning a favour" or "repaying goodwill," this expression describes the act of fulfilling one's social obligation by reciprocating help or support that was previously received. Due to the influence of Buddhism, it is believed that sooner or later, the favour needs to be returned.

These three expressions highlight the significance of 'ren-qing' in Chinese culture and the importance of reciprocity, mutual support and social obligations in maintaining harmonious relationships. Understanding these concepts and their implications can greatly enhance intercultural communication and facilitate more effective interactions with Chinese individuals and communities.

Closely related to 'renqing' is this idea of 'bao.' Both words form social norms that people have to respond to accordingly (Yau et al., 1999). The complete word of bao is baoying. The closest English translation would be reciprocity. If a person gives a favour to another, the receiver then carries the obligation to repay it. However, Chinese people believe the repayment should be made at the right time, when both givers and receivers can be benefited, rather than in an immediate manner. Also, the repayment of the favour usually should be bigger or more valuable than the one they received. When a person gives a favour, no matter if it is some sort of help or gift, they often do not have a specific purpose at the time, but they may have a general idea of establishing a long-term relationship with the receiver (Yau et al., 1999). Unlike reciprocity, baoying can be either positive or negative. It also includes the concept of karma, which derives from Buddhism and basically means that the external supernatural force, which is beyond human control, would eventually reward or punish a person or entity based on good or bad behaviour.

In the Chinese business context, understanding the concept of reciprocity and its implications for business practices is essential for foreign companies looking to establish successful partnerships with Chinese counterparts. Reciprocity plays a vital role in building trust, fostering cooperation and facilitating successful partnerships. Some key aspects of reciprocity in Chinese business practices include:

- **Gift-giving:** The exchange of gifts is a common practice in Chinese business culture, serving to demonstrate goodwill, express gratitude and strengthen relationships. Gifts should be chosen with care, considering the preferences and interests of the recipient, and should be reciprocated with a gift of similar value. During a business trip to China, a foreign executive might present their Chinese counterpart with a carefully selected gift from their home country. In turn, the Chinese executive might reciprocate with a gift that represents their region or industry, such as a traditional handicraft or local specialty.

- **Favour exchange:** The practice of exchanging favours, assistance or support is another key aspect of reciprocity in Chinese business culture. When a favour is received, it is expected that the recipient will reciprocate in some way, either by offering assistance in return or by providing support in the future. A Chinese supplier may expedite the delivery of an important shipment for a foreign client facing tight deadlines. In return, the client might prioritize the supplier's requests for future orders or provide a referral to another potential customer.

- **Hospitality and social events:** Inviting business partners or clients to social events, such as dinners, banquets or cultural performances, is an important aspect of reciprocity in Chinese culture. These events serve to build rapport, foster trust and demonstrate respect for the relationship. A Chinese company might host a lavish banquet for a visiting foreign delegation, showcasing the best of local cuisine and entertainment. In return, the foreign delegation might reciprocate by inviting the Chinese company to a similar event in their home country or by hosting a special event during their stay in China.

MIANZI AND LIAN [OR 'FACE']

According to anthropologist Ho (1944), there are two types of face in Chinese culture: '*mianzi*' (面子) and '*lian*' (脸). *Mianzi* refers to the public or social face, while *lian* refers to the private or personal face. The concept of face is complex and refers to a person's reputation, social status and dignity, and is an important aspect of interpersonal relationships in Chinese society. It is closely tied to the concepts of respect, honour and shame.

Face can be gained, lost or maintained in different ways. For example, a person can gain face by achieving a high level of education, social status or wealth. A person can lose face by committing a social faux pas, breaking a promise or being publicly criticized or shamed. Face can also be maintained by showing humility, graciousness and respect to others.

In Chinese culture, maintaining face is crucial, and people are often very aware of their own face as well as the face of others. Losing face can be a source of great embarrassment, and it can damage a person's social standing and relationships.

Face can also play a role in social interactions and communication. For example, a person may use indirect language or nonverbal cues to avoid causing offense or loss of face. Similarly, a person may give compliments or show deference in order to maintain or gain face.

In the intricate dance of international business, nowhere is the art of negotiation more nuanced than in China. As you venture into this fascinating world, you'll discover that preserving 'face' – or *mianzi* – for oneself and others is of paramount importance. The mastery of this concept can be the difference between a successful business partnership and a shattered one.

Picture this: a Chinese company is negotiating with a foreign supplier. The supplier presents terms that are unsatisfactory to the Chinese company. Instead of directly expressing their dissatisfaction, the Chinese company gracefully employs indirect language and questions to convey their concerns. This subtle approach allows the supplier to save face while addressing the issue, effectively preserving the harmony between both parties. At the same time, when the Chinese find that the foreign side is "giving face" to them, they will adjust themselves accordingly and be more helpful and friendly in the later rounds of negotiations. Therefore, it is recommended that foreign parties calculate prices and bargaining limits carefully, and always reserve certain margins for the Chinese, to allow them to gain face.

When it comes to feedback and performance evaluations, the concept of face takes centre stage once again. Direct criticism can cause individuals to lose face, posing a challenge for managers in the Chinese business context. So, imagine a manager at a Chinese subsidiary of a multinational corporation. They commend their employee's hard work and dedication before gently suggesting areas for improvement. This tactful approach ensures the employee saves face while still receiving constructive feedback.

In the realm of conflict resolution, *mianzi* reigns supreme. When disputes arise, Chinese individuals may prioritize maintaining face for themselves and others over asserting their position. For example, a Chinese employee might opt to discuss their concerns privately with a coworker or seek the help of a trusted intermediary rather than confronting the coworker directly. This approach preserves face for both parties and keeps the workplace harmonious.

In conclusion, mastering the art of *mianzi* is crucial for foreign companies seeking to establish a presence in the Chinese market. By being sensitive to the concept of face, adopting appropriate communication strategies, and demonstrating respect and humility in your interactions, you can navigate the complexities of Chinese interpersonal dynamics and foster successful relationships with your Chinese partners, clients and stakeholders.

GUANXI

Guanxi (关系) is a complex and multifaceted concept in Chinese culture that refers to the system of social networks and interpersonal relationships that facilitate business and social interactions. The word *guanxi* has been literally translated to 'relationship' in English. However, the inherent meaning of *guanxi* is more complicated than relationship. This word is composed of two characters, 'guan' and 'xi.' 'Guan' means relating while 'xi' means bonding. Thus, combining them means the social relationship between two people (Yau et al., 1999).

As mentioned previously, Chinese people must take care of immediate family. Yau et al. (1999) explained that social bonding includes relatives, people from the same town, classmates, colleagues, heirs of friends for more than two generations, people who share the same hobbies, past bosses and subordinates, people who were taught by the same teacher, past students taught by oneself, members of the same school or clan, acquaintances and friends. These bonds serve to control social behaviours in a society.

In essence, *guanxi* represents the connections and trust that individuals build over time through personal interactions, favours and reciprocity – the rénqíng that we talked about earlier. The importance of *guanxi* in Chinese society can be traced back to the influence of Confucianism, which emphasizes the significance of relationships, loyalty and maintaining harmony in society.

In the Chinese business context, *guanxi* plays a crucial role in determining the success of business transactions and partnerships. Establishing and maintaining strong *guanxi* with partners, clients, suppliers and government officials can provide companies with access to resources, opportunities and preferential treatment. Conversely, a lack of *guanxi* can hinder a company's ability to navigate the complex Chinese business environment.

Real-life examples of *guanxi* in action

- Access to resources and opportunities: Having strong *guanxi* with key stakeholders can provide companies with valuable resources and opportunities that might not otherwise be available. For example, a company with strong *guanxi* might gain access to a supplier's limited inventory, secure a favourable contract or receive an invitation to participate in a lucrative project. In the early 2000s, foreign automobile manufacturers seeking to enter the Chinese market, such as General Motors and Volkswagen, had to form joint ventures with Chinese companies. By establishing strong *guanxi* with their Chinese partners, these foreign companies were able to gain access to local knowledge, resources and government support, which facilitated their entry into the Chinese market.

- Negotiating business deals: In Chinese business culture, the process of negotiation often involves cultivating *guanxi* with potential partners or clients. This may include engaging in social activities, such as dinners or gift-giving, to build trust and rapport before discussing business matters. When Walmart was looking to expand its presence in China, it faced significant challenges due to the complex regulations governing foreign retailers. Walmart's executives invested time and effort in building *guanxi* with Chinese government officials and local partners, which helped them navigate the regulatory environment and secure the necessary permits to open new stores.

- Resolving disputes: Strong *guanxi* can be beneficial in resolving disputes and overcoming challenges in the Chinese business context. By leveraging their personal relationships, individuals can often find mutually beneficial solutions to conflicts or problems. When Apple Inc. faced a trademark dispute with a Chinese company over the use of the name 'iPad,' Apple was able to leverage its *guanxi* with key stakeholders to negotiate a settlement and avoid a protracted legal battle.

Case Study –
People or Price –
The Ericsson Approach in China

The decision-making process in Chinese businesses is deeply influenced by Confucian principles, which favour interpersonal relationships over legal contracts. This cultural trait necessitates a people-oriented approach from foreign companies. Building a high level of trust with Chinese partners is crucial, not only for successful negotiations but also as a strategy to counter any potential Chinese business tactics.

Background: This case study looks at the business strategies of the Swedish multinational, Ericsson, focusing on its negotiation processes for various telecommunications projects in China over several years. It highlights the cultural nuances of Chinese business practices, particularly the concept of '*guanxi*,' and how foreign companies can navigate this landscape.

The Case: Ericsson was in direct competition with Motorola for a project. Despite Motorola presenting a more cost-effective proposal [their license fee was US $0.5 million compared to Ericsson's US $1.5 million, and their hand phones were priced at US $1,050 against Ericsson's higher rates], the Chinese negotiators leaned toward Ericsson. This preference underscored a fundamental aspect of Chinese business culture: the emphasis on relationships over purely transactional elements like price.

Ericsson's *Guanxi* Strategy: Ericsson understood the importance of personal relationships ['*guanxi*] in Chinese business
culture. This was evident in how the Chinese value foreign visits.
When Ericsson teams hosted Chinese delegates with excep-
tional hospitality, this gesture was highly appreciated and often
reciprocated during subsequent visits to China. Such interactions
are prime opportunities for foreign companies to build rapport
and establish *guanxi* with Chinese decision-makers.

Ericsson employed a local Chinese executive who emphasized the philosophy, "To do things in China, you must do
people first." This approach was further exemplified by the use
of a 'zhongjianren,' or middleman, a Shanghainese employee
at Ericsson. This individual played a pivotal role in negotiations,
acting as a cultural and relational bridge. His involvement was
instrumental in resolving deadlocks and building trust, demonstrating that in the Chinese context, a familiar face is often more
effective than a foreign one.

Outcome and implication: In summary, Ericsson's experience
in China illustrates the critical importance of understanding and
integrating into the Chinese concept of *guanxi*. It demonstrates
that in the Chinese market, relationships and trust can be just as
significant, if not more so, than the price or the quality of the
product or service being offered.

As we can see, appreciating the importance of *guanxi* in Chinese culture and its impact on business practices is crucial for foreign companies seeking to establish a presence in the Chinese market. By investing in the development and maintenance of strong *guanxi* networks, foreign businesses can foster trust, cooperation and success in their dealings with Chinese partners, clients and stakeholders.

SUMMARY

In this chapter, we introduced three pivotal Chinese cultural words that offer profound insights into the nuances of Chinese society and culture, particularly within business and social interactions. These terms are:

- 人情 (*Renqing*): This term encapsulates the subtleties of social obligations and the exchange of favours within Chinese society.
- 面子 (*Mianzi*) and 脸 (*Lian*) (**Face**): These concepts relate to the notions of social prestige, respect and self-esteem, playing a crucial role in interpersonal dynamics.
- 关系 (*Guanxi*) (**Relationships**): This term signifies the importance of personal connections and networks in Chinese culture, underscoring the value of building and maintaining relationships.

In forthcoming chapters, we will provide practical tips and tools on how to effectively understand, master and apply these key concepts in a business context. Stay tuned for more insightful guidance on navigating the complexities of Chinese cultural dynamics in professional settings.

PART THREE

The 'HOW'

CHAPTER 9

How to Approach Common Barriers and Challenges in Intercultural Communication

By now, you have not only observed the visible aspects of Chinese communication but have also delved into its philosophical underpinnings and core values. It's now time to focus on practical actions and strategies for embracing these differences and adapting your communication style accordingly. In this final section, I will equip you with tools, ideas and tips to effectively navigate the complexities of intercultural communication with China.

We'll look at an array of frameworks and theories that can be referenced when encountering challenges in cultural differences. A central focus will be on Geert Hofstede's Cultural Dimensions Theory, which sheds light on how variations in cultural values and social behaviours influence communication. Additionally, we will tackle individual-level barriers to intercultural communication, including issues related to attitudes, perceptions, stereotypes and linguistic competence, among others. This multifaceted approach aims to provide you with a comprehensive guide to understanding and overcoming the challenges inherent in intercultural interactions with Chinese counterparts.

CULTURAL DIMENSION

Intercultural communication can be challenging. On a group level, cultural dimension theory is useful for explaining the cause of such challenges.

Cultural dimensions are frameworks that help compare and categorize cultures based on various aspects of social behaviour and values. One of the most influential frameworks in this area is Geert Hofstede's Cultural Dimensions Theory, which he developed in the late 1970s and 1980s through extensive research on national culture differences (Hofstede, 1980, 2001). Hofstede identified six primary dimensions along which cultures vary, providing a tool for understanding and comparing cultural differences in various contexts, including business.

Hofstede's six cultural dimensions are:

1. **Power Distance Index (PDI):** This dimension reflects the extent to which people accept and expect unequal distribution of power within a culture. High power distance cultures tend to have centralized authority and hierarchy, and greater acceptance of inequality, while low power distance cultures emphasize egalitarianism and shared decision-making.

   In the context of Chinese culture, which is known to have a high PDI, the acceptance of hierarchy and power differences is evident in various aspects of daily life and business practices. In Chinese culture, there is a strong emphasis on showing respect for authority figures, such as parents, teachers and supervisors. This can be observed through practices like using formal titles when addressing seniors, offering one's seat to an elder in public transportation, or presenting business cards with both hands as a sign of respect. Chinese businesses also tend to have a more hierarchical organizational structure, with clear lines of authority and decision-making power concentrated at the top levels of management. Employees are expected to follow their supervisors' instructions and may be hesitant to express dissent or offer alternative ideas out of respect for their superiors.

2. **Individualism vs. Collectivism (IDV):** This dimension assesses the degree to which people prioritize personal goals and autonomy (individualism) or the well-being of their in-group and interdependence (collectivism). Individualistic cultures value self-reliance and

personal freedom, whereas collectivist cultures prioritize group harmony and loyalty.

Chinese culture is known for its collectivist orientation. Collectivist cultures emphasize group harmony, loyalty and interdependence. For example, in Chinese culture, family is a central aspect of life. People are often taught from a young age to prioritize the needs and interests of their family over their own individual desires. Filial piety, a Confucian principle, emphasizes the importance of showing respect and obedience to one's parents and elders, and fulfilling one's duties toward the family. Teamwork and collaboration are often emphasized over individual achievements. In work settings, employees may be more likely to collaborate with their colleagues and seek consensus in decision-making, rather than pursuing their own individual goals or competing with their peers.

3. **Masculinity (MAS) vs. Femininity:** This dimension examines the extent to which a culture values traits traditionally associated with masculinity (e.g., competitiveness, assertiveness, ambition) or femininity (e.g., nurturing, cooperation, modesty). Masculine cultures tend to emphasize material success and achievement, while feminine cultures prioritize quality of life and caring for others.

   According to Hofstede, Chinese culture tends to lean more toward the masculine side of the MAS dimension, with some aspects of femininity as well. This means that traditional gender roles and values associated with masculinity are often more pronounced in Chinese society. However, some elements of the feminine dimension are also present.

   In Chinese society, traditional gender roles are still quite prevalent, with men often being expected to be the primary breadwinners and women taking on caregiving and household duties. While these roles have evolved over time and continue to change, they still exert some influence on the expectations and behaviours of individuals in the culture. Chinese work culture often places a strong emphasis on hard work, material success and achievement. Employees may be expected to work long hours, demonstrate dedication to their job, and strive for promotions and career advancement. This can lead to a highly competitive work environment, where individual accomplishments are highly valued. There is a famous Chinese expression, called '内卷' (Nèi juǎn), describing elites working hard to be even more successful.

Despite the emphasis on masculine values, Chinese culture also exhibits some feminine traits, such as a focus on group harmony, cooperation and maintaining relationships. In both personal and professional settings, maintaining harmony and fostering cooperative relationships are essential aspects of Chinese culture.

4. **Uncertainty Avoidance Index (UAI):** This dimension measures the degree to which people feel threatened by ambiguity and seek to minimize uncertainty through rules, rituals or clear expectations. High uncertainty avoidance cultures prefer structured environments and resist change, while low uncertainty avoidance cultures are more adaptable and open to innovation.

   Chinese culture typically exhibits a moderate to high Uncertainty Avoidance Index (UAI) scores, which means that the society tends to feel threatened by ambiguity and seeks to minimize uncertainty through various means. Chinese business culture tends to be risk-averse, with companies often preferring to stick with tried-and-true strategies and methods rather than venturing into uncharted territory. This can be seen in the preference for long-term planning, meticulous research and careful decision-making processes to minimize potential risks and uncertainties.

In Chinese culture, education and expertise are highly valued as a means of reducing uncertainty and achieving success. Students are encouraged to excel academically and pursue higher education to gain specialized knowledge and skills, which can help them navigate an uncertain world and secure stable, well-paying jobs.

5. **Long-Term Orientation (LTO) vs. Short-Term Orientation:** This dimension assesses the extent to which a culture values long-term planning, perseverance and future orientation (long-term orientation) or focuses on short-term goals, immediate gratification and maintaining traditional practices (short-term orientation).

Chinese culture typically exhibits a strong Long-Term Orientation (LTO) rather than a Short-Term Orientation, which means that the society places greater emphasis on long-term planning, persistence and the importance of adapting to changing circumstances. Chinese families often prioritize long-term goals, such as saving for a child's education or investing in real estate, over short-term pleasures and consumption. According to data presented by HSBC in 2019 at the World Economic Forum, parents from mainland China tend to have much earlier and longer saving plans for children's education compared to other Western societies. This long-term focus can also be seen in intergenerational planning, with adult children expected to care for their aging parents and contribute to the family's long-term well-being.

In the business world, Chinese companies often adopt a long-term perspective when making decisions and developing strategies. This can include long-term investments in infrastructure, research and development, and employee training, as well as cultivating long-lasting relationships with partners and customers.

In Chinese culture, patience and persistence are highly valued qualities, as they are seen as essential for achieving long-term success. Young children will be taught the idea of 先苦后甜 (Xiān kǔ hòu tián, "bitterness first and sweetness comes after"), 滴水穿石 (Dī shuǐ chuān shí , "dripping water can penetrate a rock"). This can be observed in various aspects of life, from mastering a new skill or pursuing an ambitious project, to navigating complex social and business relationships. Another aspect of Chinese culture's long-term orientation is the emphasis on adaptability and pragmatism. The Chinese have a saying, "crossing the river by feeling the stones," which highlights the importance of learning from experience and adapting to changing circumstances in order to achieve long-term goals.

6. **Indulgence (IND) vs. Restraint:** This dimension gauges the extent to which a culture allows the gratification of basic human desires (indulgence) or regulates and suppresses those desires through strict social norms (restraint). Indulgent cultures tend to value leisure, enjoyment and personal freedom, while restrained cultures prioritize self-discipline and restraint.

   Chinese culture tends to lean more toward the restraint side of the Indulgence (IND) vs. Restraint dimension, which means that society generally places greater emphasis on self-discipline, moderation and adherence to social norms. However, in recent years, there has been a noticeable shift toward indulgence, especially among younger generations and in urban areas.

In Chinese culture, modesty and self-discipline are highly valued, with individuals often expected to exercise restraint in their behaviour and emotions. This can be seen in practices such as avoiding public displays of affection, speaking modestly about one's achievements and exercising self-control in various aspects of daily life.

In recent years, there has been a growing trend toward indulgence in Chinese society, particularly among younger generations and in urban areas. This can be seen in the increasing popularity of consumer culture, with a greater focus on leisure, travel and luxury goods. Additionally, the rise of social media has provided new avenues for self-expression and individualism, contributing to a more indulgent and less restrained lifestyle for some.

It's unsurprising that communication challenges often arise when people from cultures positioned differently on these dimensions interact. Diverse values influence not just the content of communication, but also its timing, the involved parties and the manner of delivery. Gaining an overview of where your own culture and Chinese culture stand within these cultural dimensions can provide a general understanding of differing norms and values. Such knowledge is invaluable for navigating the complexities of intercultural communication, allowing for more effective and respectful interactions across cultural boundaries.

BARRIERS AT AN INDIVIDUAL LEVEL

Whereas we do not have control of which culture and society we were born into, there are areas we can be aware of to overcome the barriers at an individual level. Gibson (2000) pointed out five barriers to successful intercultural communication. They are attitude, perception, stereotypes, interpretation and cultural shock. I would like to add two more: linguistic competence and experience. Now let's have a look at each one in turn.

ATTITUDE

This is the easiest barrier to understand but the hardest to overcome. Rationally, we know we are different and we cannot know exactly what the other person is thinking and feeling. In Chinese, we have a famous conversation that illustrates this debate. The story is about the philosopher Zhuangzi, whom we met earlier when looking at indirect communication, and his philosopher friend, Hui Shi. One day, they were having a conversation on a bridge over a river:

> Zhuangzi: The fish are swimming freely. That is the joy of the fish.
>
> Hui Shi: You are not the fish. How do you know the fish is happy?
>
> Zhangzi: You are not me. How do you know that I do not know the fish is happy?
>
> Hui Shi: I am not known; therefore, I do not know you. You are not a fish; therefore, you do not know whether the fish is happy or not. That is all.
>
> Zhuagzi: Let us get back to your original point. You asked how I know the fish is happy. Your question assumes that I know. I got to know this on top of the bridge.

I do not know about you, but I find the above conversation fascinating. Before we get carried away by the philosophical debate, it is useful to remember that we may never fully know what the other person is thinking or saying. In other words, it is naïve to believe other people think and communicate just as you do. This is particularly the case when it comes to communicating across cultural boundaries. The right attitude in any intercultural communication is to be open and curious.

It's common to find certain situations strange, uncomfortable or even unacceptable, especially when they clash with our own cultural norms. This is exemplified in a story I recently read about an ancient Greek explorer. During his travels, he encountered a remote tribe where, contrary to his own culture's practices, the people would consume the bodies of the deceased instead of cremating them.

Intrigued, he asked a tribal son, "Why don't you burn and bury your father?" The son, horrified by the suggestion, retorted, "Why would you do such a cruel thing to my father?" Later, when the explorer returned to his Greek island, he posed a similar question about consuming a deceased father's body to a local. The response mirrored the tribal son's horror, with the Greek local exclaiming, "How could I commit such a cruel act to my father after he passes?"

This story poignantly highlights the ease with which we might regard our own practices, values and beliefs as universally correct, while perceiving those of others as erroneous. It brings to the forefront the significance of fostering an open mind and nurturing curiosity in the face of cultural differences. Being ready to learn alternative ways of thinking and doing things is contingent upon adopting the right attitude. Embracing this mindset is key to understanding and valuing the rich tapestry of global cultures.

PERCEPTION

We are all biased by our own limited understanding and knowledge of the world. Our perceptions are not the absolute truth and are not universal. This is the most common barrier of intercultural communication. Remember the story about the death ritual? Our perception determines what we believe to be the right way to behave and communicate.

This phenomenon aligns with a well-known Chinese idiom, 盲人摸象 (máng rén mō xiàng), which highlights how limited perception leads to partial understanding. The idiom originates from an ancient Indian tale involving six blind men who had never encountered an elephant. They are all keen to know exactly what an elephant looks like. They begged the emperor to allow them to touch the elephant so that they can find out. The emperor agrees to the request. The blind men went ahead to touch and feel the elephant. One shouts, "It's like a wall." The other says "No, it's like a rope." Someone else shouts, "It's a fan." They cannot agree on what the elephant looks like. As you can see from the image below, they are all wrong, as they only perceive part of the truth.

CHINESE IDIOM OF 盲人摸象

This allegory mirrors our own experiences; our perceptions are often constrained by our limited understanding and knowledge of the world. This limited perspective is a common obstacle in intercultural communication. By acknowledging the limitations of our viewpoints and remaining open to alternative perspectives, we can overcome barriers in intercultural communication and develop a more holistic understanding of our diverse world.

STEREOTYPE

Stereotyping, a term we are all familiar with, involves assigning specific attributes to all members of a group without considering individual differences. As someone from China, I've often encountered assumptions that I must be "good at maths" and possess a "strong work ethic." While I take pride in my work ethic, the stereotype about my mathematical prowess doesn't quite hold true for me.

It's important to recognize that while identifying patterns and tendencies in behaviour is a natural and necessary process for the human brain, overreliance on such categorizations, especially in the context of culture and human behaviour, can lead to oversimplification. Our brains categorize and classify information to make it more manageable, but overuse of these processes in understanding cultural and behavioural complexities can lead to underestimating the intricacies of human nature, including our communication.

While it's useful to be aware of general patterns, we must remember that everyone is unique, and broad generalizations can often mislead and hinder true understanding. It's about striking the right balance between recognizing commonalities and respecting individual differences, especially in our increasingly interconnected world.

INTERPRETATION

Gibson makes a crucial distinction between 'perception' and 'interpretation.' Interpretation involves understanding that even when we all receive the same information, we may interpret it differently. This concept is a central aspect of what's termed 'pragmatic failure' in linguistics, which describes a situation where a listener fails to accurately grasp the speaker's intended meaning.

Consider the following example, adapted from Alder (1997:70):

> A Chinese businessperson is in negotiations with a Norwegian partner. The Chinese individual remarks that the deal will be exceedingly difficult. The Norwegian partner asks how they can assist with solving any problems, but the Chinese businessperson is puzzled by this question.

The crux of the issue here is that the Norwegian partner did not correctly interpret the true, intended meaning of 'the deal will be exceedingly difficult.' In this context, the phrase was meant as a polite refusal, not an invitation for help.

This misinterpretation exemplifies one of the most challenging yet fascinating aspects of intercultural communication: the ability and awareness to understand the speaker's intended meaning. Failing to do so can lead to communication breakdowns. Accurately grasping the intended meaning can prevent embarrassment and save time and resources, highlighting the importance of nuanced understanding in intercultural interactions.

CULTURAL SHOCK

The final barrier that Gibson identifies is cultural shock, a particularly pertinent issue when relocating to a new country and adapting to a different work environment. Typically, cultural shock unfolds in various stages, as the image below indicates. It could take up to six months to fully experience the effects of cultural shock, with an additional six months required for adjustment and eventual adaptation to the new environment.

Research has highlighted the significant negative psychological effects of cultural shock. For instance, a study involving Chinese managers in the US revealed the profound impact of cultural differences. One manager recounted an incident where a US manager placed his feet on the desk during a meeting, which the Chinese manager perceived as a grave sign of disrespect and a threat to his 'face.' The experience was so unsettling that it was challenging for the Chinese manager to recover from the perceived humiliation. This example underscores the often-unintended consequences of cultural shock and the importance of intercultural communication training and awareness. Being prepared for differences and potential discomfort can help manage expectations and facilitate smoother adaptation.

Fortunately, most people eventually adapt and adjust to new cultural environments, becoming more culturally aware in the process. The inevitable struggles and misunderstandings are all part of the journey toward greater cultural understanding and competence.

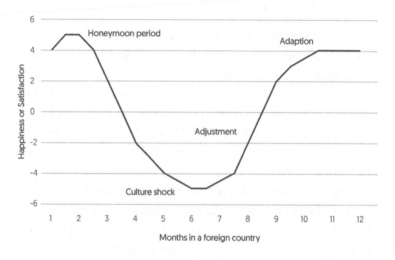

THE CULTURAL SHOCK CURVE

LINGUISTIC COMPETENCE

As an applied linguist, it may not surprise you that I believe linguistic competence is another barrier to intercultural communication. The nature of intercultural communication is such that it is likely to occur in one speaker's nonnative language. Often, it occurs in both speakers' nonnative languages. For instance, when a Chinese person communicates with a French person, they will likely speak Mandarin, French, or English – the lingua franca. In the first two scenarios, at least one party is using their native language. The chances of conveying unintended meaning in your native language are lower than when using a second language. In the third scenario, where a Chinese person speaks with a French person in English, the situation becomes more complicated, with both parties relying on their English proficiency to communicate effectively.

Another factor in communicating in your nonnative language is what we call 'pragmatic transfer,' which has two dimensions. The first is the transfer of pragmatic knowledge

– or worldview – known as 'socio-pragmatic transfer.' For example, modesty is valued in Chinese culture. The typical response to a compliment is rejection, downplaying one's achievement or the nature of the compliment. Thus, this pragmatic knowledge is transferred even when speaking a second language. Instead of a simple "Thank you," more common in English, a Chinese person might say, "Not really, it's not that good" or "No, I still have a long way to go. I must do better next time." This is not a lack of English linguistic proficiency, but the application of their own cultural pragmatic knowledge. The second dimension is the transfer of language, involving the transfer of specific linguistic expressions or patterns. For example, English speakers learning Chinese often struggle with placing time and location before the action verb. As a result, many English speakers transfer the linguistic structure of English to Chinese when they speak it. This is known as 'language transfer.'

Both pragmatic and language transfers are common for language learners and are part of the process of second language acquisition. The more you practice the language and become fluent, the better you can minimize both transfers. In situations where both speakers may still experience some level of pragmatic transfer, communication between them is likely to be challenging.

Professional translators and interpreters are invaluable in important meetings or for legal documents. However, their presence isn't always feasible, especially in international work environments. If you're considering working in China, language becomes even more crucial. A 2018 study investigating Polish expatriates in a Chinese subsidiary of a Western multinational company found that low Mandarin proficiency was a significant obstacle to socialization, leading to exclusion, social isolation, stress, frustration and negative attitudes toward collaboration with local personnel. Language barriers hindered expatriates from acquiring information from Chinese superiors, learning about team problems and participating in decision-making. Thus, pre-departure training in both Chinese language and cultural awareness is highly recommended.

When communicating in a language that is neither yours nor the other person's first language, it's important to remember that one or both of you may be influenced by pragmatic transfer. Don't hesitate to clarify if needed. Remember to be curious and open-minded.

EXPERIENCE

It may seem obvious, but it bears mentioning: a lack of real interaction with people from diverse cultural backgrounds can limit your awareness. Such a lack of exposure is a barrier, as it can lead to the belief that there is only one way of doing things. If the opportunity arises, embrace learning a new language, travel widely and consider spending a year abroad. Engaging in these activities is invaluable for building experiences that shape your attitude, enhance your appreciation of different perspectives, help overcome cultural shock, develop interpretation strategies and improve your linguistic proficiency. Essentially, each of the barriers mentioned can be addressed through intercultural communication experiences.

If such opportunities are not always feasible, explore ways to build a more international network, or seek opportunities to lead a multilingual team. Even engaging with films and novels from cultures you're interested in can be beneficial. The key is exposure, but the real game-changer is actual interaction.

SUMMARY

This chapter aims to enhance your understanding of and ability to address common challenges in intercultural communication. It underscores the importance of cultural sensitivity, self-awareness and continuous learning as you navigate the complex landscape of global interactions. I hope you have found this 'how-to' chapter beneficial. Now, let me show you more.

CHAPTER 10

How to Master Intercultural Communicative Competence

This book is designed to help you develop a critical skill in our increasingly interconnected world: Intercultural Communicative Competence (ICC). Although we're primarily focusing on cultural nuances within China, the applicability of ICC reaches far beyond any single country. It is an indispensable tool for effective and appropriate interactions across diverse cultural backgrounds. ICC is more than just language proficiency; it encompasses profound understanding, interpretation and communication with individuals from various cultures.

Now, I'll highlight the significance of ICC in numerous aspects of life, from professional settings to social gatherings. This chapter emphasizes ICC's role in preventing misunderstandings, fostering mutual respect and enabling positive interactions. It also provides you with a self-assessment tool, allowing you to monitor your own progress and development in ICC.

INTRODUCTION TO INTERCULTURAL COMMUNICATIVE COMPETENCE

First things first, what exactly is Intercultural Communicative Competence (ICC)? ICC is your toolkit for understanding, interpreting and communicating with people from an array of cultures.

And why is it important? In today's globally connected world, interactions with individuals from diverse cultures are increasingly common in various aspects of life – be it in professional settings, social gatherings or even digital spaces.

The significance of ICC is underscored by a statistic from the Economist Intelligence Unit's CEO Briefing on Corporate Priorities, which reveals that "90% of leading executives from 68 countries identified cross-cultural leadership as the top management challenge for the upcoming century." ICC plays a crucial role in preventing misinterpretations, nurturing mutual respect and fostering positive interactions.

Now, let's delve into the core components of ICC, as defined by applied linguist Michael Byram. Professor Byram outlines ICC as comprising both linguistic and intercultural competences, and identifies five critical components.

INTERCULTURAL COMMUNICATIVE COMPETENCE MODEL

First, 'attitudes.' This involves curiosity and openness, the willingness to embrace different viewpoints. Let's say you're interacting with a colleague from another country who has contrasting work practices. The attitude component of ICC would encourage you to approach this with an open mind, to see it as an opportunity to learn, rather than as a challenge.

Next is 'knowledge,' which includes an understanding of cultural specifics and the social dynamics between cultures. Imagine you're on a business trip in Japan. Being aware that business cards are given and received with both hands as a sign of respect is a simple example of the 'knowledge' component at play. You also need to know that if you are having a meal in the UK, finishing your plate shows respect to the host as it indicates that you really enjoyed the meal whereas in China, leaving some food on the plate shows your appreciation toward the host's generosity.

'Skills of interpreting and relating' is up next. This is your ability to observe a situation, interpret its cultural significance and relate it to your own cultural context. For instance, if you notice a tradition or practice in a foreign culture, being able to understand its cultural significance and draw parallels or distinctions with your own culture exemplifies these skills.

The fourth element is 'skills of discovery and interaction.' It's about your ability to acquire new cultural knowledge through interaction. For example, if you're studying abroad and join a local club or event, you're exercising these skills.

Finally, 'critical cultural awareness.' This is the ability to evaluate cultural practices and perspectives, both your own and those of others. Let's say you're participating in a discussion about gender roles across different cultures. Being able to critically evaluate the influences, implications and biases involves critical cultural awareness.

So, these are the components of ICC – attitudes, knowledge, skills, and critical awareness. In each of our cross-cultural interactions, these elements are at play. And by developing these, we can improve our ICC. I encourage you to reflect on these components in your own interactions. Are there instances where you've noticed these at work? Which aspects would you like to focus on?

DEVELOPING AND EVALUATING INTERCULTURAL COMMUNICATIVE COMPETENCE

So far, we've defined ICC and discussed different components of ICC. We also established the importance of ICC in today's global world. In this section, we will turn to the process required to develop ICC and gain an understanding of how to best measure your own ICC.

The Intercultural Competence (ICC) model by Deardorff (2004) is a widely recognized model that attempts to define the complex construct of intercultural competence. According to this model, intercultural competence is viewed as a process that leads to effective and appropriate communication and behaviour in intercultural situations. The process module of the model specifically covers the knowledge, skills and attitudes that are seen as prerequisites to achieving intercultural competence, along with the desired internal and external outcomes.

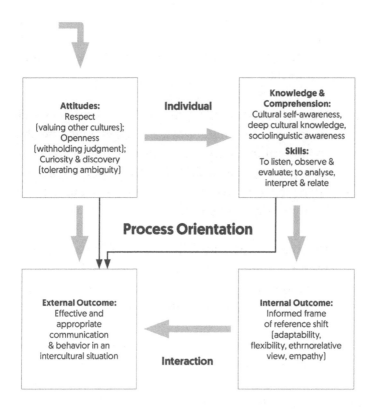

INTERCULTURAL COMPETENCE BY DEARDORFF, 2004

Here's an outline of the process module:

- **Attitudes:** Deardorff asserts that the process starts with personal attitudes such as respect (valuing all cultures), openness (withholding judgment), and curiosity and discovery (tolerating ambiguity).

- **Knowledge and comprehension:** The model proceeds to knowledge and comprehension, including cultural self-awareness, deep understanding and knowledge of culture and cultural differences (history, values, politics, economics, communication styles, etc.).

- **Skills:** This stage includes the ability to listen, observe and interpret, and the ability to analyse, evaluate and relate.

- **Desired internal outcome:** If the process goes well, the desired internal outcome is adaptability, flexibility, an ethnorelative view and empathy. This would involve being able to shift one's frame of reference and adapt one's behaviour to fit the norms and expectations of a different culture.

- **Desired external outcome:** This is effective and appropriate communication and behaviour in intercultural situations, which results in the final stage of the process model – becoming interculturally competent.

The model underlines that the development of intercultural competence is a continuous, lifelong process. One can't simply achieve intercultural competence and then stop; it's about ongoing learning, unlearning and relearning. The model also points to the importance of experience and reflection in the process of developing intercultural competence. It is also important to note that Deardorff's model allows for individual variation, which means different individuals might follow a slightly different path or place varying levels of emphasis on different stages based on their own personal experiences, cultural contexts and learning styles.

The next key question following understanding ICC is: How do we measure it? And even more importantly, how can you, as individuals, assess your own progress?

Let's begin by understanding what measuring ICC means. It's not like a mathematics test where there's a clear right or wrong answer. Instead, it's about evaluating our attitudes, knowledge, skills and awareness, the key components of ICC that we discussed in our last section.

There are several tools developed by researchers to measure ICC. These usually take the form of questionnaires or self-assessment tools. Examples include the Intercultural Development Inventory (IDI) (https://www.idiinventory.com/) and The Global Competence Aptitude Assessment (GCAA) (https://globallycompetent.com/assessment-about-the-gcaa/). These tools assess your perception and reactions to different cultural situations.

Now, how can you measure your own progress? One practical approach is self-reflection and observation. Reflect on your cross-cultural interactions. Are you demonstrating openness and curiosity? Are you trying to understand and respect cultural differences? Are you able to interpret cultural practices and draw parallels with your own culture? These are indicators of your ICC progress.

Here's a strategy: Keep a reflection journal. Document your interactions and experiences. Reflect on them through the lens of attitudes, knowledge, skills and awareness. Over time, you can revisit these reflections and track your progress.

Also, seeking feedback can be a powerful tool. Engage in conversations with peers or mentors from different cultures. Ask for their perspective on your cross-cultural interactions and openness to their culture.

Remember, improving ICC is a continuous journey. It's about gradual progress, not overnight transformation. As you interact more across cultures and reflect, you'll notice growth in your ICC.

Toolbox:
Self-Assessment Checklist

Here are some immediate actions you could take:

1. Use the provided competence measure or questionnaires mentioned earlier, so that you can assess your
   current level of competence in various aspects of intercultural communication.
2. Consider your knowledge, skills and attitudes related to
   intercultural understanding, empathy, effective communication and cultural adaptability.
3. Evaluate your strengths and areas for improvement based
   on the competence measure.

Remember that improvement takes time, and it's okay if you're not perfect at everything on this list just yet. The important thing is that you're trying to learn and improve. You should come back to this from time to time to track the progress you're making. Here's a simple self-assessment checklist:

Self-Assessment Checklist:
- **Openness:** How often do I approach new cultural settings with an open mind? Am I willing to set aside my cultural biases?
- **Knowledge:** How much do I know about the culture I'm interacting with? Have I taken steps to learn about its traditions, social norms and values?
- **Skills of Interpreting and Relating:** Can I relate practices in the culture I'm interacting with to those in my own? Can I interpret unfamiliar practices in the context of the culture they originate from?
- **Skills of Discovery and Interaction:** Am I proactive in seeking opportunities to interact with individuals from different cultures and learn from those experiences?
- **Critical Cultural Awareness:** Can I critically evaluate my own culture as well as others? Am I able to recognize cultural biases in myself and in the information I consume?
- **Reflection:** Do I regularly reflect on my intercultural interactions and try to learn from them? Am I keeping a reflection journal?
- **Feedback:** Do I seek feedback from peers or mentors from different cultures on my cross-cultural interactions?
- **Continual Improvement:** Am I aware that developing intercultural competence is a lifelong process, and am I committed to ongoing learning?

SUMMARY

In this chapter, we've focused on the essence of Intercultural Communicative Competence (ICC), drawing insights from the perspectives of renowned scholars Michael Byram and Darla Deardorff. We've illuminated the multifaceted nature of this indispensable skill in our increasingly interconnected world.

You've been introduced to the core components of ICC as well as the processes and practical tools for developing and evaluating your ICC skills. Let's remember the importance of ongoing learning, experience and reflection in the development of ICC.

Much of the chapter is dedicated to a self-assessment checklist. This tool encourages you to evaluate your own competencies in various aspects of intercultural communication.

I hope this second guide and toolbox help boost your confidence and enhance your self-awareness and self-evaluation skills in navigating the complex world of intercultural interactions!

CHAPTER 11

How to Adapt your Communication Style

The two toolboxes we've explored so far are designed to equip you with enhanced intercultural awareness. Now, we'll transition to the tools necessary for intercultural communication itself. You might be surprised to learn that this third set of tools continues to focus on you. Indeed, effectively adapting your communication style begins with being mentally prepared for it. This chapter is geared toward helping you understand and manage your own psychological aspects in intercultural communication.

You will be introduced to three crucial theories: Anxiety/Uncertainty Management (AUM) Theory, Communication Accommodation Theory (CAT), and Social Identity Theory (SIT). These theories lay the groundwork for understanding how individuals interpret and navigate cultural differences, combining psychological and social perspectives. This chapter aims to unpack these theories and their relevance to effective business communication, providing you with a robust foundation before you begin adapting your communication style for interactions with Chinese speakers.

ANXIETY/UNCERTAINTY MANAGEMENT (AUM) THEORY

Developed by William B. Gudykunst in the 1980s and 1990s, the Anxiety/Uncertainty Management (AUM) Theory explores the role of anxiety and uncertainty in intercultural communication. Gudykunst posited that successful intercultural communication is contingent on individuals' ability to manage the anxiety and uncertainty that arise from cultural differences (Gudykunst, 1988, 1995, 2005).

According to the AUM Theory, anxiety is commonly experienced when people anticipate negative outcomes or feel threatened in intercultural interactions. Uncertainty, on the other hand, refers to the cognitive inability to predict or explain the behaviour of others due to cultural differences. AUM Theory suggests that managing anxiety and uncertainty is crucial for effective communication and relationship-building across cultures.

Key principles of AUM Theory include:

1. **Mindfulness:** Gudykunst (2005) emphasizes the importance of mindfulness in managing anxiety and uncertainty. Mindfulness involves being fully present in the moment, paying attention to one's own feelings and thoughts, and being aware of others' perspectives. By being mindful, individuals can better understand their own emotions and reactions, and adapt their communication styles accordingly.

2. **Optimal levels of anxiety and uncertainty:** AUM Theory posits that there are optimal levels of anxiety and uncertainty that facilitate effective intercultural communication. Too little anxiety and uncertainty may lead to complacency, while excessive anxiety and uncertainty can inhibit communication. By striking the right balance, individuals can engage in more meaningful and constructive interactions.

How to apply AUM Theory in business:

- **Engage in Cross-cultural Training:** Consider enrolling in cross-cultural training programs, especially if you're part of an international or multicultural team. These programs, which focus on mindfulness techniques and understanding cultural differences, can equip you with the tools to navigate intercultural interactions confidently, reducing feelings of anxiety and uncertainty.

- **Prioritize Open Communication:** Always strive to create an environment where open communication and feedback are welcomed. If you ever feel uncertain about cultural nuances, or if something makes you anxious, don't hesitate to voice your concerns. Remember, it's essential to seek clarification when needed. If you're in a leadership position, be approachable and attentive, offering guidance and support to those who seek it.

- **Seek Common Ground:** Whenever you're interacting with people from different cultures, look for shared goals, interests or values. These commonalities can be a solid foundation, reducing anxiety and building trust. Participate in team-building activities or even casual social events, as they can be a fantastic way to connect with shared interests and strengthen intercultural relationships.

- **Boost Your Cultural Intelligence:** Make it a point to enhance your cultural intelligence. This ability, which involves understanding, adapting and responding effectively to various cultural contexts, can be your best tool against intercultural anxiety. Take the initiative to learn about different cultures, stay open to diverse viewpoints, and continually hone your empathy and intercultural communication skills.

In conclusion, AUM Theory provides us valuable insights into the role of anxiety and uncertainty in intercultural communication. It is reassuring to know that it is normal to feel anxious or lost at times during intercultural communication. However, applying mindfulness and a balanced approach could help with better engagement with uncertainty and cultural differences. By following these guidelines, you can confidently navigate the complexities of a multicultural environment and build more meaningful connections.

COMMUNICATION ACCOMMODATION THEORY (CAT)

Communication Accommodation Theory (CAT), developed by Howard Giles in the 1970s, is a framework that explains how people adjust their communication style based on social identity and interpersonal motives during interactions (Giles, 1973; Giles and Coupland, 1991; Giles, Coupland, and Coupland, 1991). The theory posits that individuals tend to converge or diverge their communication style to either enhance social identification and rapport or maintain social distinctiveness, respectively.

Key principles of CAT include:

1. **Convergence:** Individuals adjust their communication style (e.g., speech rate, accent or vocabulary) to be similar to their conversation partner. This strategy aims to reduce social distance, increase rapport and facilitate mutual understanding.

2. **Divergence:** Individuals accentuate the differences in their communication style to emphasize their distinct social identity and maintain social distance. This strategy can be used to assert power, maintain autonomy or express disagreement.

3. **Over-accommodation:** Occurs when an individual excessively adjusts their communication style, which may be perceived as patronizing or condescending by the conversation partner.

4. **Under-accommodation:** Occurs when an individual insufficiently adjusts their communication style, which may be perceived as unfriendly or incompetent by the conversation partner.

Applying CAT in business:

- **Practice Active Listening:** Make it a priority to cultivate active listening skills in your daily interactions. To truly understand those you converse with, focus on their verbal and nonverbal cues. Engage by asking open-ended questions and take a moment to summarize key points from discussions. This ensures both clarity and mutual understanding, resulting in more effective communication.

- **Embrace Empathy and Build Rapport:** Work on nurturing your empathy. By genuinely understanding and validating the emotions, perspectives and needs of those you interact with, you create a foundation for meaningful dialogue. Make an effort to find common ground, show genuine interest in others and consider mirroring nonverbal cues when appropriate. These techniques can significantly enhance the connections you form with colleagues.

- **Develop Cultural Sensitivity:** Develop cultural sensitivity, which will provide you with the insights to understand and appreciate the myriad cultural nuances and communication styles you might encounter.

Armed with this knowledge, you'll be better equipped to adapt your communication methods, avoid missteps and build stronger relationships with colleagues from all backgrounds.

- **Prioritize Flexibility and Adaptability:** In the diverse landscape of today's workplace, being rigid in communication won't do you any favours. Embrace flexibility and adaptability. Stay open to different viewpoints, be willing to adjust your language or tone when the situation demands, and always respect the unique communication preferences of others.

In conclusion, Communication Accommodation Theory (CAT) provides valuable insights into how individuals adjust their communication styles in response to social identity and interpersonal motives. The positive news is that we are more inclined to accommodate in any case as we are social animals. The accommodation can be both an unconscious and coconscious communicative act. By applying the principles of CAT in a business context, you can foster more effective communication, collaboration and relationships among colleagues from diverse cultural backgrounds.

SOCIAL IDENTITY THEORY

Social Identity Theory (SIT), developed by Henri Tajfel and John Turner in the 1970s and 1980s, posits that individuals derive a sense of self-concept and self-esteem from their membership in social groups (Tajfel, 1978; Tajfel and Turner, 1979, 1986). The theory seeks to explain how people categorize themselves and others into various social groups based on shared characteristics, such as nationality, ethnicity, profession or organizational affiliation. These social categorizations can influence individuals' attitudes, behaviours and intergroup relations.

Key principles of SIT include:

1. **Social categorization:** Individuals tend to categorize themselves and others into social groups based on salient attributes. This process helps simplify the social environment but can also lead to stereotyping and prejudice.

2. **Social identification:** People derive a sense of belonging and self-esteem from their group affiliations. Stronger identification with a group can lead to increased loyalty, conformity to group norms and differentiation from out-groups.

3. **Social comparison:** Individuals compare their in-groups with relevant out-groups to maintain positive self-esteem and group distinctiveness. This process can result in intergroup bias, where people favour their in-group and devalue or discriminate against out-groups.

Applying SIT in business:

- **Cultivate an Inclusive Organizational Culture:** Prioritize creating an environment where diversity is not just acknowledged but celebrated. By fostering an inclusive culture, you directly counteract intergroup biases and pave the way for healthier intergroup relations. Take actionable steps: implement robust diversity and inclusion policies, engage in continuous training and educational programs, and provide support for employees who might feel underrepresented.

- **Engage in Team-building Activities:** It's time to invest in team-building exercises that underline collaboration and mutual goals. These activities have the power to dissolve entrenched social categorizations and foster genuine connections between individuals. Whether it's group problem-solving tasks, workshops or just informal social gatherings, the aim is to bring together people from varied departments or cultural origins.

- **Master the Art of Conflict Resolution:** Intergroup conflicts are inevitable, but how you address them makes all the difference. Address such disagreements promptly and efficiently. Consider mediation, facilitate open dialogues or deploy strategies that highlight empathy and mutual understanding. By doing so, you'll maintain a peaceful workplace and curb the negative impacts of social divisions.

- **Lead by Example:** If you're in a position of leadership, recognize the influence you wield. Be the torchbearer of inclusivity, articulate the importance of diversity and champion a collective organisational identity. Your role isn't just to manage, but to inspire.

By focusing on shared objectives and values, you can forge a sense of unity, ensuring that everyone, regardless of their background, feels they belong.

In conclusion, Social Identity Theory (SIT) provides valuable insights into how individuals derive their self-concept from group affiliations and how this influences intergroup relations. By applying the principles of SIT in a business context, organizations can foster a more inclusive and harmonious workplace, where employees from diverse backgrounds can collaborate effectively and contribute to the organization's success.

GENERAL STRATEGIES FOR ADAPTING TO DIFFERENT COMMUNICATION STYLES

Adapting to different communication styles is an important aspect of developing intercultural communicative competence (ICC). We can now look at some general strategies for adapting to different communication styles.

- **Observe and Listen:** Observe and listen to the communication style of the person you are communicating with. Pay attention to their nonverbal cues, tone of voice and choice of words.

- **Positive Accommodation:** Adjust your communication style to match the communication style of the person you are communicating with. For example, if the person communicates in a direct and assertive style, you may need to adapt by being more direct in your communication. On the other hand, if the other speaker seems to be more expressive, you can also aim to communicate in a similar way.

- **Be Flexible:** Be flexible in your communication style and willing to adjust as needed. Recognize that communication styles can vary depending on the context and cultural background of the person you are communicating with.

- **Avoid Stereotyping:** Avoid making assumptions about someone's communication style based on their cultural background. Instead, focus on understanding their individual communication style.

- **Ask Questions:** Clarify any misunderstandings to better understand the communication style of the person you are communicating with. This will help you adapt your communication style to better fit their needs.

- **Practice Active listening:** Try giving your full attention to the person you are communicating with. Avoid distractions and focus on the message they are trying to convey. Empathy is the ability to understand and share the feelings of others. When adapting to different communication styles, practice empathy by putting yourself in the other person's shoes and trying to understand their perspective.

- **Build Rapport:** Building rapport with the other person can help you adapt to their communication style. Find common ground and use it to build a connection with the other person. This can help to build trust and improve communication.

Overall, adapting to different communication styles requires a combination of observation, flexibility and active listening. By following these strategies, you can develop the skills needed to effectively communicate with people from different cultural backgrounds.

SUMMARY

This chapter offers a comprehensive guide to adapting your communication styles in diverse cultural settings, by helping you manage your own psychology.

By understanding and applying the principles of AUM (Anxiety/Uncertainty Management), CAT (Communication Accommodation Theory), and SIT (Social Identity Theory), along with general strategies for communication adaptation, you will be able to enhance your intercultural communicative competence. This is pivotal for fostering more effective, empathetic and respectful interactions, whether in personal or business contexts.

CHAPTER 12

How to Communicate Effectively with Chinese People

Having now acquired all the general tools for developing your intercultural communicative competence and preparing mentally to adapt your communication styles, it's time to shift our focus to specific tools for effective engagement with China. This chapter offers practical advice for successful communication with your Chinese clients or partners in business environments.

Building on the discussion of Chinese communication styles in Chapter 4, we delve deeper into understanding and adapting to the nuances of Chinese communication, encompassing both verbal and nonverbal aspects. This chapter underscores the importance of respecting cultural norms, grasping the concept of high-context communication, and recognizing the subtleties of nonverbal cues that are integral to Chinese business culture.

HOW TO UNDERSTAND CONTEXT

In previous chapters, we've established that Chinese communication is highly contextual. Sometimes, failures in intercultural communication are not due to a single element, but rather a compound effect influenced by many contextual factors. Do you recall the story from Chapter 1? It involved two groups of six Chinese engineers visiting their British business partner, with each meeting yielding drastically different outcomes. This scenario is drawn from a comparative study conducted in 2004 by Professor Helen Spencer-Oatey and Xing, examining two Chinese-British welcome meetings.

The table presented below outlines the key similarities and differences between these two meetings. At first glance, the differences might appear minor. Most people, when asked which meeting was more successful, tend to choose the second one, primarily because it was shorter and seemed smoother, with no noticeable waiting periods.

However, the reality was quite different. The second meeting had a detrimental effect on the relationship between the Chinese and British firms. The visiting delegations were so displeased that they cancelled all their planned training sessions, choosing to go sightseeing instead for the remaining 10 days of their visit.

	Meeting 1	Meeting 2
Seating	British chair at front, Chinese guests, and British hosts on each side	Same layout as meeting 1
Duration/ Structure of the welcome meeting	Longer due to pre-meeting waiting.	Shorter; timings were smooth as no one was kept waiting. Pre-meeting was very brief.
	No offer to the Chinese visitors to deliver a speech in return.	No offer to the Chinese visitors to deliver a speech in return.
Chairman	Sales and Marketing manager for China	Operations Director
Interpreter	No formal interpreter: the researcher helped.	A local Chinese technical expert acted as an interpreter
Chinese visitors	Six engineers	Six engineers

SIMILARITIES AND DIFFERENCES BETWEEN MEETING 1 AND 2

So, what exactly went wrong in the second meeting? The researchers identified a range of contextual elements that contributed to its failure. Let's examine these elements one by one.

A key factor was the status of the engineers in each delegation. While both groups consisted of six engineers, those in the second group also held significant managerial roles within their company, such as sales manager and division director.

On a Chinese business card, it is common to see two titles. One title typically reflects the individual's expertise, such as senior engineer or professor. There's also the position title, which indicates the person's actual role in the organization, such as general manager or dean of an academic department. In this context, the position title is more significant, as it denotes the status and seniority of the individual within the organization.

The failure to recognize the seniority of the second Chinese delegation by the British hosts led to unintended consequences. While the same seating arrangement was suitable for the first delegation, it failed to convey equal status and respect to the more senior second delegation. Additionally, not offering a chance to deliver a speech in return caused offence to the second group. The self-perceived seniority of this delegation implicitly demanded and expected a different kind of treatment and arrangement, which is normal in a hierarchical culture like China's but was overlooked by the British host.

Another contextual factor was the significant deal the Chinese company had signed with the British one. The Chinese side believed this deal was pivotal for the British company. From their perspective, the partnership should have been highly valued and acknowledged, which wasn't the case in the British chair's speech, leading the Chinese to perceive the British as arrogant and ungrateful.

Ironically, the long wait for the British chair in the first meeting facilitated small talk, an essential component in building rapport and trust. Though the British saw this as merely filling an awkward silence, the Chinese valued it as an opportunity for relationship building. The British chair's extensive travel experience in China, compared to the chair of the second meeting who had never been to China, also played a role in the differing outcomes of the meetings.

The final straw was the role of the interpreter in the second meeting. After the British chairman's speech, when the Chinese head of delegation tried to give a speech in return, he was interrupted by the interpreter, who insisted they simply introduce themselves. This action, seemingly innocuous, was perceived as disrespectful by the Chinese delegates, as they believed such behaviour wouldn't have occurred without the British chair's endorsement.

The Chinese delegates' perception of their own status and importance heightened their sensitivity to 'face' issues. Aspects like seating arrangements, the lack of opportunity to give a speech in return and the nature of the British chair's welcome speech all became issues of 'face.' People from diverse cultural backgrounds place different levels of importance on small talk and have varied ways of building relationships. To understand relationship management in intercultural contexts, insights into the social expectations and judgments of the involved parties are essential.

As this case study demonstrates, many contextual factors can contribute to challenges in intercultural communication. So, how can we develop strategies or skills to identify the context? While it's impossible to be prepared for every communication situation, in each case, you can analyse the context using a framework. The SPEAKING model is a useful framework for understanding key elements in communication contexts.

THE SPEAKING MODEL

The SPEAKING model was introduced by linguist and anthropologist Dell Hymes in 1974. The model aims to aid fieldworkers in their attempt to document and analyse instances of language use. To me, his model provides a perfect tool for also evaluating the context of any intercultural communication that you are going to enter. It is a valuable model for preparing important communication such as meetings and negotiations.

The identification and labelling of the components of linguistic interaction was driven by Hymes' view that, to speak a language correctly, one needs not only to learn its vocabulary and grammar, but also the context in which words are used.

The model has 16 components that can be applied to many sorts of discourse: message form; message content; setting; scene; speaker/sender; addressor; hearer/receiver/audience; addressee; purposes (outcomes); purposes (goals); key; channels; forms of speech; norms of interaction; norms of interpretation; and genres.

Hymes constructed the acronym SPEAKING, under which he grouped the 16 components within eight divisions. The acronym SPEAKING stands for Setting and Scene, Participants, Ends, Act Sequence, Key, Instrumentalities, Norms, and Genre. Let's gain an understanding of each key division.

- **Setting and Scene:** The setting refers to the time and place where the communication takes place and, in general, the physical environment. The board meeting may be a setting for an important business meeting. The scene is the 'psychological setting' or 'cultural definition' of a setting, including characteristics such as range of formality, and sense of play or seriousness. The board meeting where company performances and future direction are discussed tend to be formal and serious. This could be different if it is a post-work social in a local bar – the setting is more relaxed and casual.

How to apply this: Consider the physical and social context in which the communication takes place. Within intercultural settings, the setting might involve a diverse range of cultural backgrounds, languages and social norms. Be aware of how these factors influence the communication process and adapt accordingly, such as by choosing a neutral location or being sensitive to cultural preferences regarding personal space and seating arrangements.

• **Participants:** The British welcome meetings could have gone much better if the speakers and audience had been researched more carefully. As discussed earlier, speaker and audience carry statuses in the participation framework. Understanding the expectation of their roles and status helps when choosing your words. At a board meeting, the chairman is expected to enjoy certain rights and fulfil responsibilities according to cultural conventions and norms.

How to apply this: Analyse the roles, relationships and social statuses of the individuals involved in the communication. Intercultural communication often involves people with different expectations, values and communication styles. Recognize these differences and adjust your behaviour accordingly, such as by using appropriate forms of address, making an effort to pronounce names correctly and being mindful of nonverbal cues.

- **Ends:** This refers to the purposes, goals and outcomes. What do you want to get out of the interaction? Gain trust? Reach a deal? Is it to find out more about the counterpart? Also, what would the other party want to get out of this interaction with you? What do they need to achieve? By having this in mind, it allows us to deploy different linguistic strategies accordingly. At a wedding, the best man may tell a story about the groom to entertain the audience and affirm the love between the groom and the bride. At a board meeting, the CEO may be required to provide a financial report to update and reassure investors.

  How to apply this: Identify the goals or objectives of the communication, which may differ across cultures. In intercultural settings, it's essential to be aware of how different cultures prioritize various communication goals, such as building relationships, sharing information or negotiating agreements. Adapt your communication style to align with these goals and demonstrate respect for cultural values and preferences.

- **Act Sequence:** This is the form and order of the event and refers to how something is said about message form and what is said regarding message content. A best man's speech might start with funny stories about the groom and end with a toast and best wishes to the newly wedded couple. The audience might laugh during the speech and would surely applaud at the end of the speech. For a business meeting in the UK, an agenda is circulated in advance to ensure the act sequence is planned. In other countries, like China, a more fluid approach may apply. For example, a meeting may involve a topic for discussion. The order of the discussion is less spelled out.

Usually, the person who calls for the meeting will chair and manage the discussion.

How to apply this: Consider the structure and organization of the communication, which can vary across cultures. In intercultural communication, be aware of cultural differences in conversational patterns, turn-taking, and the use of silence or indirectness. Adjust your own communication style to better align with these patterns, while also being patient and open-minded when encountering unfamiliar or unexpected conversational styles.

- **Key:** This refers to the clues that establish the 'tone, manner or spirit' of the speech act. The best man might imitate the groom's voice and gestures in a playful way, or he might address the group in a serious voice, emphasizing the sincerity and love the speech expresses. In a tough negotiation in the boardroom, the tone may be more assertive.

How to apply this: Analyse the tone, mood or manner of the communication, which can be influenced by cultural norms and expectations. In intercultural settings, be sensitive to cultural differences in the use of humour, formality, politeness and emotional expressiveness. Adapt your own communication style to respect these cultural norms and be prepared to adjust your expectations when encountering different communication styles.

- **Instrumentalities:** These are the forms and styles of speech. The channel of the communication determines the style of the speech. It would be strange if a wedding speech was presented in a written format and equally, it would be strange if a financial report was not.

How to apply this: Consider the channels and forms of communication used, such as verbal, nonverbal, written or digital communication. In intercultural communication, be aware of potential language barriers and cultural variations in nonverbal cues, gestures and facial expressions. Learn key phrases or cultural gestures, and be mindful of potential miscommunications or misunderstandings due to language or nonverbal differences.

- **Norms:** These are the social rules governing the event and the participants' actions and reaction. In a playful team social event, the norms might allow many audience interruptions and collaboration. A serious, formal financial report at the board meeting will call for paying attention to the CFO and no interruptions.

  How to apply this: Identify the social rules and expectations governing the communication process. Intercultural communication often involves navigating different cultural norms and values, such as rules around politeness, punctuality and gift-giving. Educate yourself about these norms and demonstrate respect for them in your interactions, while also being flexible and understanding that others may not be familiar with your own cultural norms.

- **Genre:** This refers to the kind of speech act or event. Different disciplines develop terms for kinds of speech acts, and speech communities sometimes have their own terms for types.

How to apply this: Recognize the type of communication, such as a formal presentation, casual conversation or business negotiation. In intercultural settings, be aware of cultural differences in the expectations and conventions associated with various genres, such as the use of storytelling, visual aids or the role of audience participation. Adapt your communication style to suit the genre and cultural context, and be open to learning from new or unfamiliar communication traditions.

By applying the SPEAKING model in intercultural communication settings, you can gain a deeper understanding of the complex dynamics at play, improve your communication skills, and foster more effective and respectful interactions across cultures. Before you go into an important meeting or negotiation with Chinese counterparts, using the SPEAKING model as a checklist. It helps you take each aspect of communication into consideration and navigate the context of the communication.

OTHER CONSIDERATIONS FOR HIGH-CONTEXT COMMUNICATION

In addition to being attentive to the context of communication, I recommend considering the following four areas to enhance your effectiveness in communicating with Chinese business colleagues. These actions encompass adopting the right attitude, focusing on specific areas of learning and establishing a supportive network.

- **Be patient and respectful:** As we have learned, Chinese business culture places a strong emphasis on hierarchy and respect. Show deference to senior individuals and be patient during negotiations, as the decision-making process might be slower than in Western business culture. Take the time to understand the cultural nuances and adapt your communication style accordingly.

  Example: When the Walt Disney Company was negotiating the establishment of the Shanghai Disney Resort, it encountered several challenges related to high-context communication. Disney needed to navigate complex relationships with local government officials, business partners and other stakeholders, which required patience and adaptability (Huang and Qian, 2018). During the negotiations, Disney's executives often engaged in elaborate banquets and gift-giving ceremonies to build rapport and trust with their Chinese counterparts, demonstrating the importance of understanding high-context communication in Chinese business culture. However, their patience and effort eventually paid off and the Shanghai Disney Resort became a great success.

- **Gain knowledge of cultural references:** Familiarize yourself with common Chinese idioms, proverbs and metaphors used in business communication. Understanding these cultural references can help you better comprehend the messages being conveyed and demonstrate your respect for Chinese culture.

  Example: A foreign executive received a message from their Chinese counterpart that included the idiom "crossing the river by feeling the stones" (摸着石头过河, mōzhe shítou guò hé). By understanding that this idiom refers to a cautious and pragmatic approach to problem-solving, the foreign executive was able to appreciate the Chinese partner's suggestion to proceed slowly and carefully with a new project, avoiding potential risks and pitfalls.

- **Invest in language learning:** While many Chinese businesspeople speak English, learning some Mandarin can be beneficial in building rapport and showing respect for your Chinese counterparts. Even basic language skills can help break down barriers and create a more comfortable atmosphere during business interactions. If you were planning to work and live in China, as discussed earlier, then this becomes essential both in terms of your professional responsibilities and your personal social wellbeing. Chinese business communication frequently employs metaphors, idioms and proverbs to convey complex ideas. These expressions often have deep cultural and historical roots, so understanding their meaning requires contextual knowledge of Chinese culture and language (Hu, Grove, and Zhuang, 1991).

  Example: A foreign executive who frequently travelled to China for business decided to take Mandarin lessons.

Over time, the executive was able to engage in simple conversations with Chinese partners and colleagues, which greatly improved the rapport and trust between them. The language skills also helped the executive better understand the cultural nuances during meetings and negotiations.

- **Leverage local expertise:** If you are not well-versed in Chinese business culture, consider partnering with local experts or hiring employees with experience in the Chinese market. They can provide valuable insights and guidance on how to navigate the complexities of Chinese high-context communication and business practices.

  Example: Uber's initial entry into the Chinese market was challenging, partly due to a lack of understanding of local business culture and practices. To address this, Uber hired local managers with extensive experience in the Chinese market, such as Liu Zhen, a former executive at Baidu and Tencent. By leveraging local expertise, Uber was able to better navigate the Chinese market and adapt its strategy to local preferences.

I have now outlined some key considerations for communicating with China, acknowledging its nature as a high-context culture in the business arena. It's evident that by understanding and adapting to Chinese communicative styles, foreign companies can forge strong relationships, prevent misunderstandings and ensure successful business interactions in China. Developing cultural awareness and refining communication skills can offer a significant competitive edge in the rapidly expanding Chinese market. Remember, all good things require time, so it's important to be patient and adopt a long-term perspective.

NONVERBAL COMMUNICATION

The nonverbal communication aspect is as critical as the spoken word, if not more. Respect, hierarchy and harmony are essential elements that are often communicated through nonverbal cues. What are the specifics you should know when it comes to nonverbal communication with China in business context?

- **Handshake:** As a greeting, the handshake is the most prevalent style in Chinese business contexts. This applies to initial meetings as well as to subsequent encounters when the relationship has become more established. It is also gender-neutral. One study that examines comparative perspectives from Chinese and European managers on business negotiation includes an anecdote about a Chinese businesswoman's first meeting with her French host. She felt upset because her host did not shake her hand. Only later did the Chinese businesswoman learn that in France, men typically wait for women to offer their hand first before shaking it. This example is intriguing, as it demonstrates that intercultural communication is indeed a two-way street and essential in avoiding misunderstandings.

- **Business Card Exchange:** This is a crucial ritual in Chinese business culture. The card should be presented with two hands and the text facing the person receiving it. When receiving a business card, it's polite to study it carefully for a moment before placing it in a business card case. Placing it directly into a pocket or bag is considered disrespectful. Along with reading the business card, it is common to give compliments to the person's achievements by highlighting their titles.

You can also express your delight to meet them in person if you have interacted with them previously but haven't had the opportunity to meet them.

- **Bow or Nod:** Traditionally, a slight bow or nod is a common way to greet someone, though handshakes are increasingly popular. The senior person generally initiates the handshake, and it's common to stand closer to each other compared to Western standards. Make sure you smile warmly when you nod to indicate agreement or approval.

- **Eye Contact:** During a meeting or conversation, Chinese businesspeople might not maintain constant eye contact, but avoiding it entirely can be perceived as a sign of evasion or disrespect. Chinese individuals might signal that they are listening attentively by taking notes or looking downwards. If this occurs, don't take offence. A speaker might choose to emphasize their attentiveness by deliberately looking away. This stems from the Chinese cultural belief that by reducing one sense, another can be enhanced. By avoiding visual distractions, one might listen more effectively.

- **Body Language:** Overly expressive body language or gestures are typically avoided in Chinese business settings to maintain an atmosphere of control and respect. It's advisable to adopt a calm and composed demeanour.

- **Seating Arrangements:** In meetings, the seating arrangement often denotes hierarchy. The seat at the head of the table is reserved for the most senior or most respected person. It's best to wait until you're directed where to sit. At a dinner table, the same rule applies.

- **Personal Space:** In crowded cities and public places, the concept of personal space can be different from Western norms. However, in business settings, personal space is still valued, and unsolicited physical contact is usually avoided.

- **Gift Giving:** This is often part of doing business in China, but it needs to be done with care to avoid inadvertently violating taboos. Gifts should be offered and received with both hands, like business cards. Cultural knowledge is important here. Don't give yellow or white chrysanthemums because they are associated with funeral and sadness. Don't offer clocks, as they are associated with death. You should also avoid using white or black gift-wrapping paper – unless it's Chanel! Red and gold are colours of good luck and glamour. And remember – don't give green hats, especially to males.

- **Silence:** Silence is valued in Chinese communication. It's seen as a chance to reflect and think. Therefore, do not rush to fill the silence in business meetings.

SUMMARY

This chapter offers a comprehensive guide to navigating the intricacies of communication within Chinese business settings. You are reminded of the importance of understanding the context in Chinese communication. We can see from the case study how seemingly minor differences in approach and perception can significantly impact business relationships. We've discussed the SPEAKING model, introduced by

Dell Hyme, as an invaluable tool for dissecting and under-standing the various elements of communication in different settings. This model helps in breaking down the complexi-ties of intercultural communication by focusing on various aspects such as the setting, participants, ends, act sequence, key, instrumentalities, norms and genre.

We have also looked at other considerations for effec-tive communication in Chinese business culture, such as the virtues of patience and respect, the benefits of famil-iarizing oneself with cultural references and idioms, and the advantages of language learning and leveraging local expertise. These aspects are crucial for foreign businesses to establish strong, respectful and successful interactions with Chinese counterparts. Finally, we've looked at examples of the nuanced nonverbal communication norms in China, such as the ritualistic nature of business card exchanges, subtleties of body language and the careful observance of seating arrangements.

This chapter serves as an insightful resource, equipping you with the knowledge and skills necessary to adeptly nav-igate the nuanced landscape of Chinese business communi-cation. Whether it's through understanding nonverbal cues, appreciating the high-context nature of communication or applying the SPEAKING model, this chapter provides valu-able strategies for fostering effective and respectful business relationships in China.

How to Build Successful Interpersonal Relationships and Rapport with Chinese People

After working on how to decode context and adapt to Chinese communication styles, let's now focus on how to build successful interpersonal relationships and rapport with Chinese people. Since we know it is not only a necessity but also a strategy to nurture strong and meaningful relationships in Chinese business culture, this chapter builds on the earlier discussion on key cultural concepts like *renqing* (人情), *guanxi* (关系), and *mianzi* (面子) in Chapter 8, and aims to offer practical tips on navigating interpersonal dynamics in China. The intricate interplay of these concepts significantly influences business communication and practices, so understanding them is essential in the Chinese business environment. This is 'how to win friends and influence people' – Chinese style!

HOW THE THREE CONCEPTS ARE INTERCONNECTED

Before we discuss what to do to build successful interpersonal relationships with Chinese people in business contexts, let's recap the three key cultural words and have a better understanding of how they are interconnected.

- *Renqing* **as the foundation for** *guanxi*: *Renqing* plays a crucial role in building and maintaining *guanxi*. By participating in the exchange of favours and adhering to the norms of reciprocity, individuals can strengthen their personal connections and expand their *guanxi* network. For example, a Chinese businessperson might offer assistance to a potential partner, expecting that the favour will be returned in the future. This exchange of *renqing* helps to solidify their *guanxi*, fostering trust and cooperation.

- *Mianzi* **and** *guanxi*: Preserving *mianzi* is a key element in maintaining strong *guanxi*. By demonstrating respect, humility and sensitivity to the face of others, individuals can nurture their personal connections and create a harmonious atmosphere. For instance, a Chinese manager might avoid directly criticizing an employee in front of others to protect the employee's face, thereby preserving the *guanxi* between them.

- *Renqing* **and** *mianzi* **in conflict resolution:** In the event of a dispute or disagreement, *renqing* and *mianzi* can guide conflict resolution. By prioritizing the preservation of face and fulfilling the obligations of *renqing*, parties can work toward a resolution that maintains harmony and strengthens their *guanxi*. A real-life example of this can be found in a case study by Yau, O. H. M. (1994), which highlights how a Hong Kong-based company resolved a dispute with a Chinese partner by offering a face-saving solution that satisfied the *renqing* obligations of both parties.

In summary, *renqing*, the exchange of favours, forms the basis of *guanxi*, the network of personal connections. Maintaining *mianzi*, or social standing, is crucial for preserving these connections, often involving tactful communication and respect. Lastly, *renqing* and *mianzi* together play a pivotal role in conflict resolution, where face-saving solutions that honour social and reciprocal obligations can strengthen *guanxi*. Now let's take a close look at how you can take care of each aspect in your business interactions.

HARNESSING THE POWER OF *'RENQING'*: STRATEGIES FOR THRIVINGIN THE CHINESE BUSINESS ARENA

Imagine the scene: A bustling marketplace in Beijing, where vibrant colours, rich aromas and the lively chatter of merchants and customers fill the air. At the heart of this energetic exchange lies the principle of *renqing*, masterfully guiding the ebb and flow of social interactions. Let's look at some of the strategies and tips to develop and apply *renqing* in Chinese business contexts:

- **Cultivate the tradition of gift-giving:** In the intricate dance of Chinese business relationships, gifts play a starring role. Exchanging tokens of appreciation at meetings, holidays or celebrations is not merely a pleasant custom; it is an integral expression of *renqing*. In a study by Luo et al. (2012), researchers found that gift-giving played a crucial role in fostering trust and cooperation between Chinese and American businesspeople.

  Tip: Before meetings or significant events, invest in thoughtful tokens such as high-quality tea or fine wine. Remember, it's not about the price but the intent behind the gift.

- **Host or partake in culinary celebrations:** The clink of glasses and the savoury aroma of exquisite dishes signal the delightful union of business and pleasure. The convivial atmosphere of the feast allows for subtle negotiations and quiet understanding, fostering trust and collaboration.

Tip: Invite business partners or potential clients to traditional banquets. This not only showcases generosity but also provides a relaxed atmosphere for discussions and negotiations.

- **Offer assistance and seek it in return:** Actively look for opportunities to aid partners or colleagues in any capacity you can. In the vibrant tapestry of Chinese business life, acts of kindness and support are threads of gold.

Tip: Whether it's sharing market insights or providing resources, such acts embody *renqing* and foster mutual reliance. Remember, today's assistance can sow seeds for tomorrow's partnerships.

- **Hone the art of delicate communication:** The power of *renqing* shines brightly in the delicate art of Chinese communication. Chinese business interactions often value implied meanings and indirect communication. Like a master calligrapher, the Chinese communicator carefully chooses words to maintain harmony in relationships.

Tip: Take time to learn local expressions and idioms, and be patient. Sometimes, what's not said is as important as what is. A refusal might come in the form of a gentle deflection rather than a direct 'no.'

- **Build a robust network:** In China, your connections are your most valuable asset. Introducing like-minded individuals and forging new alliances is not only a strategic move – it is a reflection of *renqing* in action.

Tip: Attend local networking events, join business associations or partake in community activities. By introducing people or businesses that can benefit from each other, you're enacting *renqing* and solidifying your own position within that network.

To navigate the Chinese business landscape, *renqing* isn't just a concept, it's a practice. By integrating these strategies, not only will you resonate with the local business ethos, but you'll also pave the way for long-lasting, fruitful partnerships in this ancient and dynamic culture.

ALWAYS MAINTAIN AND PROTECT 'FACE' NEEDS

Understanding the importance of *mianzi* is essential for foreign companies aiming to succeed in the Chinese market. By being sensitive to the concept of face and adopting appropriate strategies, you can build stronger relationships, foster cooperation and minimize misunderstandings. Here's how:

- **Deciphering ambiguous nodding and understatements:** A challenge you might encounter when working with Chinese colleagues is their tendency to nod and affirm understanding with "yes, yes, yes," even when they might not fully comprehend. This behaviour, often rooted in a desire to save face, suggests they might be reluctant to admit confusion, particularly in public settings. In these scenarios, it's important to approach the situation with sensitivity.

  Tip: Gently repeat your points or seek clarification. Preferably, do this in a private setting or follow up with an email, to avoid putting the person in an uncomfortable position.

- **Embrace a diplomatic communication style:** Employ tactful language and avoid direct criticism. Express concerns or disagreements in a polite and respectful manner. On the other hand, do not shy away from compliments, which can enhance the face needs of your Chinese colleagues.

  Tip: Ensure that you wait for a formal introduction in group settings. This maintains the respect and dignity of all parties involved. If conflicts arise, handle them privately rather than in front of a group. Chinese culture tends to be collective, so never assume that criticizing one individual will be perceived as such. It is highly possible that it could be perceived as dissatisfaction with the entire company or deal. Publicly pointing out mistakes can cause a significant loss of face to many.

- **Show respect and humility:** Demonstrate reverence for the opinions, concerns and expertise of your Chinese partners, clients and employees. Ensure the correct seating arrangement is made. Provide the opportunity for equal speaking time in formal situations.

  Tip: Recognize hierarchy and titles: In Chinese business culture, hierarchy is paramount. Addressing individuals with their proper titles can go a long way in preserving face. Be punctual: Time is respected in Chinese culture. Being late can be seen as a sign of disrespect, which can result in a loss of face. Be aware of cultural taboos: Certain actions or topics can be considered inappropriate or unlucky. Familiarize yourself with these to avoid causing unintentional offense.

- **Be sensitive to nonverbal cues:** Pay close attention to body language, facial expressions and tone of voice to understand the underlying messages and emotions in interactions. Adjust your responses accordingly.

- **Engage in face-enhancing behaviours:** Offer compliments, acknowledge achievements and show genuine interest in the well-being and success of your partners, clients and employees.

> **Tip:** Always express appreciation for hospitality, advice or assistance provided. This can go a long way in maintaining and enhancing the face of your hosts. Presenting gifts is common practice and can enhance face.

Li Ka-shing, the renowned business tycoon, has a unique approach to hospitality and respect, which serves as a masterclass in the subtle art of Chinese face-giving. Imagine being invited to lunch at his office. As you step out of the lift, rather than being directed to a dining room or waiting area, you are met by Mr Li himself. That's right – he waits for you *outside the lift* to extend a personal greeting.

It doesn't stop there. During significant company dinners, Li Ka-shing doesn't just stay seated at the head of the table. He actively moves around, dedicating 10–15 minutes to converse with each guest, ensuring everyone feels valued by receiving his personal attention. This practice isn't merely about honouring his guests; it's a strategic way of bestowing 'face' or respect, a deeply rooted concept in Chinese culture. In doing so, not only does he enhance the esteem of his guests, but he also solidifies his reputation as a gracious and considerate leader.

So, the next time you consider business etiquette, think of Mr Li. It's not just about following traditions; it's about understanding the nuances that make all the difference.

DEVELOP AND NURTURE YOUR *GUANXI*

Chinese do not shy away from mixing personal relationships and business. Personal stories, shared hobbies and life experiences often find their way into business discussions. A Chinese businessperson might share tales of their childhood, their latest travels or even their passion for watercolour painting. Why? To build a bridge of understanding and friendship (Chen, 1997; Yum, 1991). These narratives send a clear message: "I'm not just here for business; I'm here to build a genuine connection."

According to Chen and Chen (2004), *guanxi* is a developmental process. The authors propose a process model that outlines the stages of *guanxi* development, including initiation, cultivation, maintenance and deterioration. Two key lessons from their work: 1) *Guanxi* development is a long-term game; 2) If you don't maintain *guanxi*, you will lose it.

The main role of *guanxi* is to build trust, access resources and navigate complex business environment with the help from locals. Some practical implications include:

- **Investing time and effort in building *guanxi*:** Cultivating strong *guanxi* with Chinese partners, clients, suppliers and government officials should be a priority for foreign companies operating in China. This may involve engaging in social activities, exchanging favours and demonstrating commitment to long-term relationships. Chinese people do this too and create most of their work and professional relationships through social interactions with new partners. In the supervisor-subordinate *guanxi* research, *guanxi* activities outside the work setting were used as indicators of strong *guanxi* quality.

Tip: Rather than viewing business interactions as one-off transactions, approach them as opportunities to establish lasting ties. Remember, trust is a cornerstone of *guanxi*, and it's cultivated over time. Personal relationships and business are deeply intertwined in China.

- **Leveraging *guanxi* for business success:** Foreign companies should recognize the potential benefits of leveraging their *guanxi* networks for business purposes, such as gaining access to resources, securing favourable deals or resolving disputes. However, it is essential to approach *guanxi* with genuine intentions and respect for Chinese cultural values, as superficial attempts to exploit *guanxi* for personal gain can be counterproductive.

  Tip: Approach *guanxi* with sincerity. Any inauthenticity or attempt to exploit these relationships for mere personal gain can damage your reputation and trustworthiness.

- **Navigating the complexities of *guanxi*:** While *guanxi* can provide valuable advantages in the Chinese business context, it can also be a complex and challenging aspect of doing business in China. Foreign companies should be prepared to navigate the intricacies of *guanxi*, including understanding the appropriate ways to give and receive gifts, managing expectations around reciprocity, and maintaining a balance between personal and professional relationships.

  Tip: Be aware of the stages of *guanxi* development. Know when to initiate, how to cultivate, the best practices for maintenance and the signs of deterioration. This will guide you in managing the equilibrium between personal and professional ties.

The evolution of the Chinese economy and society significantly influences business culture. As China embraces the horizontal structure of a market economy, the role of *guanxi* in accomplishing tasks subtly diminishes. Foreign companies are increasingly able to utilize the market for resource acquisition or for marketing their products and services, rather than relying extensively on intermediaries and favours, as was customary in the past. This shift does not imply that *guanxi* has become irrelevant in the maturing Chinese market. Rather, its role is evolving, potentially serving more as a facilitator than an essential element in international business dealings within China. Many scholars maintain that *guanxi*, having been shaped and reinforced over two millennia of Chinese feudal society, remains deeply ingrained in Chinese culture.

In the workplace, *guanxi* is extremely important for managing relationships, particularly upwards. Various studies (Hu, Hsu, and Cheng, 2004; Zhang and Yang, 1998) have demonstrated that workers who have better *guanxi* with their supervisors tend to receive higher rewards in China. Therefore, if you have a Chinese boss, it is in your interest to develop strong *guanxi*. Conversely, if you manage Chinese staff, don't be surprised if they invite you out for a meal at their own expense, or offer to take you to a show. Through these gestures, they are attempting to build *guanxi* with you.

SUMMARY

Chapter 13 serves as a comprehensive guide for foreign professionals looking to successfully navigate the complex landscape of Chinese business culture. The chapter emphasizes the importance of understanding and integrating the concepts of *renqing*, *guanxi* and *mianzi* into business interactions.

Mastering the nuances of *renqing*, *guanxi* and *mianzi*, and understanding their interconnections, equips foreign business professionals with the key to unlocking successful and harmonious business relationships in China. By embracing these cultural concepts and integrating them into your business practices, you pave the way for fruitful and long-lasting business partnerships in this vibrant and dynamic market.

CHAPTER 14

A Pinch of Salt – The Complexity of Culture

Thank you for staying with me to this final chapter of the book. You have developed a good understanding of the relationship between language, culture and communication. You have also been shown the cultural iceberg of China and its communication characteristics. You have been given a range of toolboxes, from awareness to mental readiness, from adapting your communication style to decoding contexts and building strong interpersonal, business relationships. My job is almost done, but there is one last thing.

While there are many advantages of viewing China through a national lens, providing a macro perspective that simplifies the country's vast complexities for easier understanding and strategic planning, you must also be cautious against the risks of overgeneralization. No single narrative can fully capture the diverse and intricate nature of such a vast and varied country. Let me explain this further.

ADVANTAGES AND RATIONALE OF DISCUSSING CHINA AT THE NATIONAL LEVEL

One cannot overlook the benefits of analysing China as a cohesive, national entity. In a world that often seeks overarching narratives and frameworks, understanding China at a national level offers a macro lens, helping to shape policies, business strategies and broader intercultural understanding.

This approach serves as an essential starting point. It simplifies the vast complexities of the Chinese context into manageable segments, facilitating easier navigation of its economic, political and sociocultural landscapes. However, it is important to be aware of the risks inherent in generalization. This is the 'pinch of salt' I'd like you to bear in mind.

CHINESE SOCIETY:
A COMPLEX MOSAIC

China's society is far from monolithic. Stretching from the urban streets of Shanghai to the rural pathways of Yunnan, from the snow-capped peaks of Tibet to the bustling markets of Guangzhou, China presents a tapestry of peoples, languages, traditions and ways of life. The Han majority coexists with 55 recognized ethnic minorities, each with its own languages, traditions and cultural nuances. This heterogeneity serves as a reminder that a one-size-fits-all approach to understanding and communicating with the Chinese can be both misleading and ineffective.

Gao and Prime's study on UPS in China and its intercultural challenges includes an insightful quote from Jim, a 57-year-old US expatriate working at UPS:

"Do not form opinions too quickly. When you come to China, when you first see things, you really have to say that it happens at this place, at this time. China is not one country; it's many countries, both in time, space and in social class. The Chinese culture is not three-dimensional; it's probably seven-dimensional, with geographical regions multiplied by historical eras." [P.152]

This highlights the importance of not assuming that macro-Chinese cultural models can completely apply to a group of Chinese from a specific region or particular race/ethnicity. It is crucial to interact with Chinese people with an open mind, avoiding stereotypes.

Another consideration is individual differences. Everybody interprets and embodies cultural elements in unique ways. This diversity stems from myriad personal experiences, backgrounds, education, familial upbringing and personal beliefs. It's akin to each person having a distinct prism through which they perceive and interact with cultural norms and values. For example, two employees from the same company might understand the organization's culture differently based on their departments, roles or past work experiences. Acknowledging these individual differences is paramount, as it reminds us that even within shared cultural frameworks, there is a spectrum of interpretations and responses. Hence, to truly understand culture, we must not only focus on the collective but also appreciate the subtleties of individual perspectives.

THE EVER-EVOLVING NATURE OF CULTURE

Change is the only constant, and Chinese culture is no exception. From the ancient dynastic eras to the modern People's Republic of China, Chinese culture has constantly evolved, absorbing, adapting and reshaping influences both foreign and domestic. With the rapid technological, economic and societal advancements in recent decades, this pace of change has only accelerated. This dynamic nature of culture emphasizes the need for continuous learning and adaptation in our approaches to intercultural communication.

PEELING BACK
THE LAYERS OF CULTURE

While examining an organization's culture from a national perspective can be advantageous in grasping overarching corporate narratives, one must understand that every organization is a subculture, with its unique ethos, values and practices. This broad view can provide a foundation for policymaking and setting universal standards. However, it's essential to tread cautiously and avoid painting all organizations with the same brush.

ORGANIZATIONAL CULTURE: A UNIQUE ECOSYSTEM

Every organization, be it a multinational conglomerate or a local start-up, has its distinct culture, shaped by its mission, leadership, history and the collective experiences of its members. This culture might sometimes align with the nation's predominant values but can also diverge, reflecting a blend of influences and strategic choices.

REGIONAL CULTURE: BEYOND NATIONAL BOUNDARIES

In a world increasingly defined by globalization and interconnectivity, regional culture often trumps national culture. For instance, the business practices and attitudes in the Asia-Pacific region may have more in common with each other than with the rest of their respective nations. Recognizing these regional nuances is crucial for organizations looking to expand their footprint and cultivate meaningful connections in new territories.

INDUSTRY CULTURE: THE UNSEEN CURRENT

Beyond organizational and regional cultures lies another influential layer: industry culture. Each industry has evolved its distinct ethos and modus operandi. Driven by historical advancements, regulatory environments, market demands and innovation patterns, industry cultures dictate unwritten rules, set standards and determine the pace at which businesses operate within them. For instance, the breakneck speed and constant innovation of the tech world contrast starkly with the steadiness and stringent regulatory compliance of the pharmaceutical industry. Recognizing and navigating these industry-specific nuances can significantly impact an organization's strategy, communication approaches and success. It's like navigating a river; while every boat (organization) might have its design and destination, the current (industry culture) plays a crucial role in determining its journey.

Grasping these layers is akin to understanding the rings of a tree – each ring tells a story, a year of growth, challenges faced and the environment's influence. To communicate effectively with the Chinese, one must be prepared to venture beyond the surface, to ask questions, listen actively and, most importantly, remain open-minded and adaptable.

Case Study:
The Fuyao Factory –
A Study in Intercultural
Communication with China

Introduction: In 2014, China's Fuyao Glass Company, responsible for 70% of China's auto windshields and windows, ventured into America's industrial heartland by opening a factory in a disused General Motors plant in Dayton, Ohio. The documentary, *American Factory*, released in 2019 by Netflix, chronicled the journey.

Objective: To explore the intercultural communication challenges experienced by the two distinct groups of employees – Chinese and American.

Background: The Dayton factory was established in a city previously symbolic of American industrial might, but which had suffered significant job losses when General Motors shut down. The introduction of Fuyao promised new employment opportunities, particularly attracting many former GM workers. Fuyao also imported a substantial number of Chinese staff, primarily for technical guidance and supervision.

Cultural Differences Observed:

1. **National/Ethnic Culture:** There were inherent cultural attitudes and practices observed among the Chinese and American workers. The Chinese workforce was depicted as diligent, resilient and disciplined, traits not as prominently highlighted in the American workers.

2. **Workplace/Industrial Relations Culture:** This refers to the culture arising from management styles, institutional frameworks and worker awareness. Fuyao's approach to this differed considerably from what the American workers were accustomed to.

Key Intercultural Challenges:

1. **Addressing National Cultural Gaps:** There was a concerted effort by management from both sides to bridge cultural differences. For instance, adapting to local labour laws and addressing Chairman Cao Dewang with respect showcased this endeavour. Workers also attempted to bridge the gap, often successfully, despite the inherent hierarchy and language barriers.

2. **Addressing Workplace Culture:** With the Chinese management in a dominant position, the onus fell on them to develop a hybrid workplace culture. The company tried to balance disparities, notably in the payment structure where Chinese workers, despite their higher skill levels, were paid less than their American counterparts.

3. **Shift in Management Perspective:** Over time, Chairman Cao Dewang and his team, particularly the new manager, Jeff, began emphasising nationalistic ideologies, causing a rift between the two groups. The subsequent pressure to meet production targets and conform to the Chinese style of work led to growing resentment among the American workforce.

4. **The Unionization Challenge:** The film highlighted Chairman Cao's anti-union stance, a stark difference from the American tradition of union representation. When workers attempted to unionize, the management adopted strong anti-union strategies, further widening the cultural and operational divide.

Conclusion: While initially there was hope for a merger of the two cultures and the birth of a cross-national, class-based culture of labour solidarity, strategic decisions by Chinese management prevented this. Instead of a genuine hybridization of cultures, there was a dominance of the 'colonizing' Chinese managerial culture over the 'colonized' American worker culture. The nuances of these cultural differences and their impacts underscore the importance of understanding and navigating intercultural communication in a globalized world.

SUMMARY

In conclusion, while a macro understanding has its merits, it is paramount to appreciate China's rich tapestry and avoid generalizations. Effective communication with the Chinese – as with any culture – requires nuance, empathy and a profound appreciation of its multifaceted nature. As we move forward, let us approach intercultural interactions with curiosity, respect and a willingness to understand, always taking singular narratives with a pinch of salt.

Understanding China at a national level can provide valuable insights for policymaking and business strategies, yet it is crucial to explore the deeper, more nuanced aspects of Chinese culture. Remember, China is a complex mosaic of diverse ethnicities, languages and traditions, and these layers of diversity must be acknowledged in any intercultural communication and engagement.

It is also important to recognize individual differences within the same cultural framework and the dynamic nature of culture, which is continually evolving and adapting. Organizational, regional and industry cultures add additional dimensions to the national culture, each influencing communication and interaction in unique ways.

This final chapter is a call to approach intercultural interactions with an open mind, respect and a readiness to learn and adapt. It encourages embracing the multifaceted nature of culture with curiosity and understanding, reminding us that singular narratives are often insufficient in capturing the richness of any culture, especially one as diverse as China's.

Epilogue

As we reach the conclusion of our journey through the complex and vivid world of intercultural communication with China for business, it feels akin to standing atop a vast wall, surveying a landscape rich in cultural depth and intricacy. This book has been more than just a guide – it has served as a lantern, illuminating the serpentine pathways and hidden alleys of Chinese culture, language and communication.

In Part One of our odyssey, we unearthed the bedrock of Chinese communication. We delved into the rich tapestry of the Chinese language, uncovering its unique thought patterns and communication styles. We ventured into the digital realms of China, exploring the all-encompassing influence of platforms like WeChat and their transformative impact on business interaction.

Part Two of our journey took us deep into the essence of Chinese communication. We explored core values shaped by ancient philosophies such as Confucianism, Taoism and Buddhism, and unravelled the meanings behind key cultural words, each a vital piece of the grand mosaic of Chinese communication.

In Part Three, we translated our newfound insights into practical wisdom. We learned to navigate the challenging waters of intercultural communication, mastering the intricate dance of communicative competence. We adapted our styles to resonate with our Chinese counterparts and wove threads of robust, meaningful relationships in the realm of Chinese business. The final chapter served as a gentle yet compelling reminder to embrace the diverse hues and nuances of Chinese culture and communication.

For those interested in learning Mandarin Chinese, I have some free resources to share. During the Covid-19 pandemic, I started a YouTube channel named '字espresso,' dedicated to teaching Chinese through morphology. To me, this aspect of the Chinese language is fascinating – revealing much about our history, ways of thinking and beliefs. Feel free to check it out at https://www.youtube.com/c/字espresso.

This journey has revealed that effective communication with China is an art form, rich in subtleties and nuances. It's about tuning into the symphony of underlying cultural values, beliefs and norms orchestrating behaviour and communication. This journey calls for patience, empathy and an insatiable curiosity to learn and adapt.

The path to mastering intercultural communication with China is ever-evolving, adorned with continuous learning and discovery. The insights and skills you've acquired are not mere tools; they are golden keys to unlocking doors of cross-cultural understanding and collaboration.

In the wise words of an ancient Chinese proverb, "Learning is a treasure that will accompany its owner everywhere." May the treasures you've discovered in these pages be your faithful companions, guiding you through the bustling marketplaces, serene gardens and majestic boardrooms of your future endeavours in the enchanting world of business with China.

During this journey, I, too, underwent my own intercultural adaptation. I struggled with settling on 14 chapters, as 14 is an unlucky number in Chinese culture, associated with death. My editor suggested merging two chapters to make it 13 in total. However, I questioned, "Isn't 13 an unlucky number in the UK?" We both laughed, and I decided not to be overly superstitious. So, this book comprises 14 chapters! Perhaps the next one will have eight chapters – for both good luck and less work.

Thank you for joining me on this enlightening expedition. Here's to your future journey, filled with boundless learning, understanding and success as you navigate the rich tapestry of intercultural communication with China. The next book in the series will focus on politeness from a Chinese perspective, another crucial dimension for developing personal and business relationships with China. I look forward to bringing you on that journey very soon.

Bibliography

Barnlund, Dean C. *Public and private self in Japan and the United States: Communicative styles of two cultures*. Tokyo: The Simul Press, 1975.

Chen, Guo-Ming. "An Examination of PRC Business Negotiating Behaviors." Paper presented at the annual meeting of the National Communication Association, November 1997, Chicago. ERIC Document Reproduction Service No. ED422594.

"Chinese Scripts and Symbols," Crystalinks, accessed 21 February, 2024, https://www.crystalinks.com/chinascript.html

Deardorff, Darla K. *International Educator*. Vol. 13. (2004).

Fang, Tony. "Negotiation: The Chinese style." *Journal of Business & Industrial Marketing* Vol. 21 No. 1, (2006): pp. 50-60. https://doi.org/10.1108/08858620610643175

Franz, Boas. *Race, Language and Culture*. New York: The Macmillan Company, 1940.

Gao, Hongmei and Prime, Penelope. "Facilitators and Obstacles of Intercultural Business Communication for American Companies in China: Lessons Learned from the UPS Case." *Global Business Languages* 15 (2010): Article 10. http://docs.lib.purdue.edu/gbl/vol15/iss1/10

Ge, Gao and Ting-Toomey, Stella. *Communicating effectively with the Chinese*. Sage Publications, 1998.

Ge, Jianqiao, Peng, Gang, Lyu, Bingjiang, Wang, Yi, Zhuo, Yan, Niu, Zhendong, Hai Tan, Li, Leff, Alexander P. and Gao, Jia-Hong. "Cross-language Differences in the Brain Network Subserving Intelligible Speech." *PNAS* Vol. 112 No. 10, (2015): pp. 2972-2977. https://doi.org/10.1073/pnas.1416000112

Gibson, Edward. "The dependency locality theory: A distance-based theory of linguistic complexity." *Image, Language, Brain*. (2000): pp. 95-126.

Giles, Howard, Taylor, Donald M. and Bourhis, Richard. "Towards a Theory of Interpersonal Accommodation through Language: Some Canadian Data." *Language in Society* Vol.2 No. 2 (1973): pp. 177–92. doi:10.1017/S0047404500000701

Greenwood, George. "Lack of Mandarin speakers raises fears for future diplomacy." *The Times*, 30 August, 2022. https://www.thetimes.co.uk/article/fears-for-china-diplomacy-as-foreign-office-reveals-shortage-of-mandarin-speakers-bkvt0bcfm

Gudykunst, William. *An Anxiety/Uncertainty Management (AUM) Theory of Effective Communication: Making the Mesh of the Net Finer*. Sage Publications, 2005.

Gudykunst, William and Young Yun, Kim. *Methods for Intercultural Communication Research. International and Intercultural Communication Annual, Volume VII*. Sage Publications, 1984.

Hagemann, Julie Ann. "Confucius Say: Naming as Social Code in Ancient China." Paper presented at the Annual Meeting of the Conference on College Composition and Communication (37th, New Orleans, LA, March 13-15, 1986). https://nla.gov.au/nla.cat-vn5470200

Hall, Edward T. *Beyond Culture*. Garden City N.Y.: Anchor Press, 1976.

Hofstede, Geert. *Cultures and Organizations Software of the Mind*. New York: McGraw-Hill, 2005.

Hofstede, Geert. "Culture's Recent Consequences: Using Dimension Scores in Theory and Research." *International Journal of Cross Cultural Management* (2001): pp. 11-17. https://doi.org/10.1177/147059580111002

Hu, H.H., Hsu, W.L. and Cheng, B.S. "Rewards Allocation Decisions of Chinese Managers: Influence of Employee Categorization and Allocation Context." *Asian Journal of Social Psychology* Vol. 7 No. 2, (2004): pp. 221-232.

Ji, Li-Jun Ji , Nisbett, Richard E. and Su, Yanjie. "Culture, Change, and Prediction." *Psychological Science* (2001): pp. 450-456. https://doi.org/10.1111/1467-9280.00384

Knapp, Mark L., Hall, Judith A. and Horgan, Terrence G. *Nonverbal Communication in Human Interaction* (2013).

Lakoff, George. "Some Remarks on AI and Linguistics."*Cognitive Science* (1978): pp. 267-275.

Nie, S. Resignation letter to department director. In Z. Feng (Ed.), *A comprehensive reader of social interactions: Volume 3* (2003) pp. 167–167. Shanghai, China: Cultural Books.

Schwartz, Shalom H. "A theory of cultural values and some implications for work." *Applied Psychology: An international review.* (1999): pp. 23-47.

Smutkupt, Suriya. "A Descriptive Study of Thai Nonverbal Communication." *Dissertations and Theses* (1976): 2587. https://doi.org/10.15760/etd.2584

Suleiman, Michael W. "Attitudes of the Arab Elite Toward Palestine and Israel." *American Political Science Review* Vol. 67 No. 2 (1973): 482–89. doi:10.2307/1958778.

Wierzbicka, Anna. *Understanding Cultures Through Their Key Words: English, Russian, Polish, German and Japanese.* Oxford University Press, 1997.

Wilczewski, Michał, Søderberg, Anne-Marie and Gut, Arkadiusz. "Intercultural Communication within a Chinese Subsidiary of a Western MNC: Expatriate Perspectives on Language and Communication Issues." *Multilingua* Vol. 37 No. 6 (2018): pp. 587-611. https://doi.org/10.1515/multi-2017-0095

Whorf, Benjamin Lee. *Language, Thought, and Reality: Selected Writings of Benjamin Lee Whorf.* Ed. John B. Carroll. Cambridge, MA: MIT Press, 1956.

Wierzbicka, Anna and Winter, Werner. *Cross-Cultural Pragmatics: The Semantics of Human Interaction.* Berlin, Boston: De Gruyter Mouton, 1991.

Xiang, Catherine Hua. *Mastering Chinese: The Complete Course for Beginners.* 1st ed. Bloomsbury Master Series (Languages). Red Globe Press, 2018.

Yau, Oliver H. M., Chan, Tsang Sing and Lau, Kelly. "Influence of Chinese Cultural Values on Consumer Behavior." *Journal of International Consumer Marketing* Vol. 11 (1999): pp. 97-116.

Zaharna, R. S. "Understanding cultural preferences of Arab communication patterns." *Public Relations Review* 21 (1995): pp. 241-255.

Zhang, Ting, Maktoba, Omar and Collins, G. Ntim. "The Joint Effects of Information and Communication Technology Development and Intercultural Miscommunication on International Trade: Evidence from China and Its Trading Partners." *Industrial Marketing Management* 89 (2020): pp. 40–49.

Zhang, Z.X. and Yang, C. F. "Beyond Distributive Justice: The Reasonableness Norm in Chinese Reward Allocation." *Asian Journal of Social Psychology* Vol. 1 No. 3 (1998): pp. 253-269.

About the Author

Dr Catherine Hua Xiang is an established author and applied linguist. She is East Asian Languages Coordinator at London School of Economics (LSE) and Programme Director of LSE's BSc International Relations and Chinese course. Catherine is the UK Director of LSE Confucius Institute for Business London. She is also a consultant to companies wishing to engage with China.